The Way You
Wear Your Hat

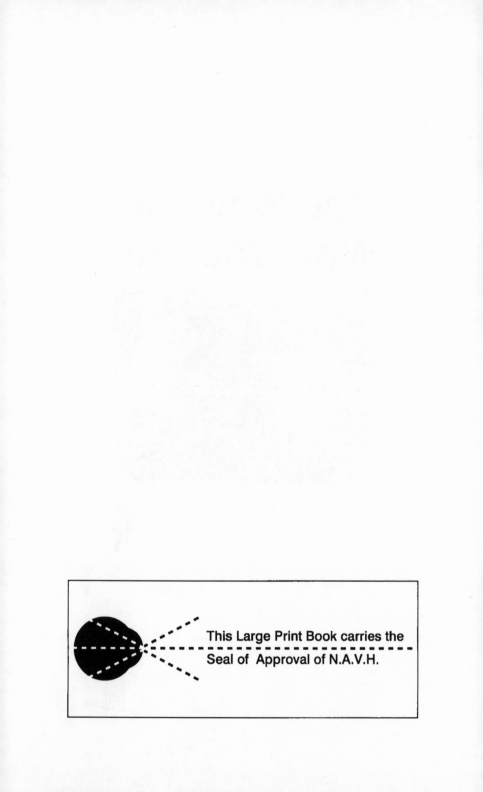

This Large Print Book carries the
Seal of Approval of N.A.V.H.

The Way You Wear Your Hat

and the Lost Art of Livin

Bill Zehme

PHOTOGRAPHS BY PHIL STERN

Thorndike Press • Thorndike, Maine

Published in 1998 by arrangement with
HarperCollins Publishers, Inc.

Thorndike Large Print ® Basic Series.

The tree indicium is a trademark of Thorndike Press.

The text of this Large Print edition is unabridged.
Other aspects of the book may vary from the original edition.

Set in 16 pt. Plantin by Minnie B. Raven.

Printed in the United States on permanent paper.

Library of Congress Cataloging in Publication Data

Zehme, Bill.
    The way you wear your hat : Frank Sinatra and the lost
art of livin' / by Bill Zehme ; photo editor, Vincent Virga ;
photographs by Phil Stern.
      p. (large type) cm.
    Originally published: 1st ed. New York : HarperCollins
Publishers, c1997
    ISBN 0-7862-1437-6 (lg. print : hc : alk. paper)
    1. Sinatra, Frank, 1915–   — Anecdotes. 2. Singers
— United States — Anecdotes. 3. Popular music —
United States — History and criticism. 4. Large type
books. I. Title.
[ML420.S565Z44   1998]
782.42164′092—dc21
[b]   98-12897
                                          MN

For **CLS** and **FAS**

. . . How dull it is to pause,
to make an end,
To rust unburnish'd, not to shine in use!
— TENNYSON

Let's start the action!
— SINATRA

Contents

WEE SMALL

"*A fella came up to me the other day with a nice story. He was in a bar somewhere and it was the quiet time of the night. Everybody's staring down at the sauce and one of my saloon songs comes on the jukebox. 'One for My Baby,' or something like that. After a while, a drunk at the end of the bar looks up and says, jerking his thumb toward the jukebox, 'I wonder who he listens to?' . . .*"

This concerns a YOUNG MAN *whose* CHICK HAS JUST SPLIT. *She flew the coop . . . with* ANOTHER GUY *and* ALL THE BREAD, *and left him with five gallons of some* VERY BAD *sweet muscatel wine from the San Joachim Valley or Old Hee-Ho. Consequently, in order to become* a winner, this FELLA *proceeds to get himself* PROPERLY BOMBED, *grabbin' the grape for about five days. He's* FRACTURED, *stoned; he's* gassed, NUMBSVILLE. *It's his* ONLY WAY OUT. *He can't figure it out sensibly. Then he decides one morning, at* ABOUT ONE OR TWO A.M., *to come out and get among the mainstream to see if he can live with us again. He's looking for* SOMEBODY TO TALK TO. *It's obvious that he's got a lot of* PROBLEMS. *And it's all summed up in* TWO WORDS: A BROAD. *Now let's face it — wars you can win. Hitler you can beat,* but NOT A DAME. *Oh, it's* murder, *doc, I tell you —* moider! *(Shake hands with the vice-president of the club!) Now, he doesn't want* ANSWERS, *he just wants to speak his piece. Finally, near* CLOSING TIME, *he falls into a small,* DIMLY LIT BAR, *a very tiny place, where a pianist is playing quietly in a corner. And the* BARTENDER *is his victim. So if you will now assume the position of the bartender, you'll hear* HIS TALE . . .

— SALOON SOLILOQUY,
A COMPOSITE SKETCH FROM
A THOUSAND NIGHTS

ALONE, WHERE DOES ONE GO IN THE DARK NIGHT OF THE SOUL?

"Wake up! . . .
You know what loners are:
Losers."

𝒥rank Sinatra did not like to be alone. Alone, he was anxious, even a little fearful. Alone, he was not himself. And if he were not himself, all loners would be lonelier, more lost, without a beacon. Irony: "Did you hear the story about the fellow who was walking around New York?" he would say, starting a favorite joke that haunted him always. "The town gets hit with an A-bomb — how's that for an opener? — and he's the only man left. He's walking around, takes four or five days, and he's finally lonely. There's nobody to talk to. So he goes up to the remains of some tall building — and he goes over the side. He's passing the sixteenth floor — and that's when he hears a phone ring." That joke never really got laughs, but the point resonated hard.

He would never be that guy.

And so, for only the lonely, he sang the rhetorical question: *"When you're alone, who cares for starlit skies?"* Not him, that's who. When he was alone, night was a bitch, a black hole, a bitter void. Night required company, required fortification and re-inforcements. Since the forties, he would not take on the night, any night, single-handedly. So he marshaled troops to sit with him, to drink and to smoke and to laugh with him. "The thing Frankie doesn't seem to understand is that the body's got to get some sleep," a bedraggled friend complained four decades ago. At that mo-ment, the *New York Times* declared: "He fights a relentless battle against sleeping be-fore sun-up." Even in the sixties, messing around on his cockamamie two-way radio, he gave himself the handle "Night Fighter."

The fight never ceased, not ever.

Sleep: dullsville, numbsville, weakness. He wouldn't even do it on airplanes. Awake, he was aware, which was all. *Be aware,* he always told Nancy Jr., had the words inscribed on her St. Christopher medal, on her first keychain. "It's the number one priority," she says.

He would break more dawns than most mortals. Each one was his triumph, the death of each night. He had survived yet another one. "He feels reborn in the morning light," his daughter Tina once attested. When horizons brightened, he exulted over the spoils of war. "Look at the colors!" he would say, pointing bleary comrades toward thousands of sunrises. "What kind of blue would you call that?" He called the tint of sky that offered him most peace Five O'Clock Vegas Blue. "You have to see it to know it," he dared disbelievers. Steve Lawrence, who saw his share of Vegas Blue, says, "I've told him he's probably the last of the Italian vampires."

How Frank did it: POWER NAPS sustained him. Long ago, he learned to doze on band buses rumbling across lost highways. After that, planes notwithstanding, he could do it anywhere, anytime, sitting up, and still maintain the creases in his tuxedo trousers.

WHAT IS A
PERFECT TOAST
FOR LATE-NIGHT
CONSOLATION?

> "Here's to absent friends —
> fuck 'em!"

*W*oe to those missing. More woe to those who greeted dawns by his side. It is there that scores of men slumped, trapped, for he insisted nobody leave. They could not hit the hay before he did, and they had to drink apace with him until the finish. It is a sore, but proud, subject among them all. They groan, lovingly, when they speak of it. Hank Cattaneo, who oversaw all technical aspects of the later concert years, would recall, "By four in the morning, I'd had enough Jack Daniel's, so I got a bartender to color Coca-Cola with water so he'd think I'm still with him." Sinatra usually caught on anyway, for he was omniscient in this area: Road manager Tony Oppedisano, or Tony O., nearly half the Old Man's age, around him for the last decade, says, "I've been with him nights where he put away a gallon of booze, and I wasn't too far behind him. He made sure. Because every once in a while he'd say,

14

'How's your drink? Let me taste it.' That way he knew it wasn't iced tea."

Begin to nod off, he would say, "Hey! What are you doing? Wake up!" Rise from the table, he would say, "Where the hell are *you* going?"

Best excuse: "To the bathroom." "Well, that's all right then," Frank would allow, if suspiciously. Big lovable Jilly Rizzo, who ran Frank's favorite New York joint and later traveled everywhere with him, would always use it as his exit line and disappear. Others took advantage of the Sinatra code of chivalry: If a woman in the group decided to retire for the night, most every man present, excluding Frank, would leap to his feet and offer to escort her safely to the door of her hotel room. Often they pushed and shoved

FS holds court, al dente

each other, vying for their out. But many who crept away were summoned back. "God help you if he knew what room you were in," says Cattaneo. "Frank himself would light firecrackers outside your door."

That was road life of the not too distant past. But even in the fifties and sixties, even in his plush Palm Springs compound, men sought escape; swell house guests like Yul Brynner and David Niven and Humphrey Bogart and screenwriter Harry Kurnitz and publisher Bennett Cerf and film producer Armand Deutsch, they wanted bed with a vengeance. Deutsch recalls, "We were a sleepy, potentially mutinous crew with a resolute host who kept an eagle eye on all the exits. Bennett, ever the pragmatist, came up with the solution. We would rotate. Two of us each night would stay the distance. It was not perfect but it worked well enough." Kurnitz, whom Sinatra believed to be the funniest man he knew, once said, "Frank is the only person I know who invites you to a black-tie party and, as he is hanging up the telephone, says, 'BE SURE TO BRING YOUR SUNGLASSES.' "

Kurnitz called Frank the Balding Prince, much to his amusement. Toward the end of his life, when the screenwriter had grown frail, he would make trips west and stay at the Beverly Wilshire Hotel. Sinatra would go there and drag him out of bed at eleven at night for wee-hour revels. Concerned, Deutsch told Frank, "You're gonna kill him! You're really gonna kill him!" And Frank replied, "No, Armando, I'm keeping him alive."

SALOON STORY, LATE EIGHTIES: He got the comedian Tom Dreesen up one night. Dreesen, who spent twelve years opening for and hanging with him, was a Palm Springs guest that night, drifting off in one of the bungalows on the Sinatra property. "Let's go get a drink," said Frank. So they drove to a saloon called Chaplin's, owned by Charlie Chaplin's son.

Dreesen recalls: "There was no one in the joint. Just one guy way in the corner, and Frank and me standing at the bar. The bartender was wrapping things up for the night. We were talking for a few minutes, when a woman, about sixty-five years old, came running into the bar. She said, 'Excuse me! Excuse me! Do you have a jukebox in here?'

"Frank Sinatra turned around and looked her right in the face and said, 'I'm sorry, what did you say?' She repeated, 'Do they have a jukebox in here?' Frank looked around the room and he said, 'No, I guess

17

not.' Then, as an afterthought, he said, 'But I'll sing for you.' And she said, 'No thanks.' And she turned around and walked out.

"What's funny was, he watched her walk out the door with this kind of sad look on his face. But he had a little smile. I said to him in that sort of awkward silence, 'She obviously didn't recognize you.'

"And he shrugged and said, 'Maybe she did.' "

TO DROWN SORROW, WHERE SHOULD ONE JUMP FIRST AND BEST?

"Certainly not water.
Water rusts you."

*I*t began thusly: Head low, heart lower, he turned to the maestro of matters wet — he turned to Jackie Gleason. It was one of those mothery Manhattan nights in the early forties and they were ensconced not at Toots Shor's, where their credit ballooned perilously; they had come instead to a joint called the Harlequin. Maybe it was a broad,

18

maybe it was business gone sour, but he smarted badly and needed something for it. "I feel like getting smashed," said Frank. "All right," said Gleason, who implicitly understood all such circumstances. Determined, Frank quietly tapped the bar top and asked, "Now what's a good drink?" Gleason gave him the withering eye: "You mean you've never gotten smashed?" Impossible but true: Sinatra shrugged no. Gleason bellowed: "JACK DANIEL'S! That's a good place to start!"

Few would be the nights thereafter that Jack did not touch his lips and balm his soul. Nineteen sixty-one: "We'd like to sing a suicide song for you now, ladies and gentlemen," he said onstage at the Copa Room in the Sands, introducing "Here's That Rainy Day," a lament so woeful as to destroy a guy. "We sold that album for $4.98, complete with a .22-caliber automatic. Except when you pulled the trigger, Jack Daniel's would come out of it. I had the fullest ears in town, with Jack Daniel's."

Together they traveled the world, a man and his sour mash whiskey, ten cases in every cargo hold beneath him, lest any foreign destination be without supply. Steve Lawrence would come to call him Jack's Original Test Pilot, which he liked. GASO-

LINE is the word Frank fondly used for it. As in: "Let's have some more gasoline!" That cry was heard across dawns immemorial, wherein pallies encircled him, emulated him, tipping in kind. "If you don't like Jack Daniel's, he looks at you like you were queer or something," attested one such pally, anonymously, in 1957. Any man who drank it was his friend. Sammy Davis Jr. did, with Coke — a desecration, the Leader thought, but in the right ballpark at least. Call for it in his presence and his face would light up. Then he would seat you beside him and refill your glass. For his singular devotion, the distillery rewarded him with what would be one of his proudest possessions — his own private acre of Lynchburg, Tennessee, ground, the soil on which the ambrosia cooks.

He would tell this story on many of those amber-drenched nights: He had gone to a new doctor who inquired about his alcohol intake. Frank stated, "I have thirty-six drinks a day." The doctor told him to be serious. Frank said that he was serious and that he drank a bottle of Jack Daniel's every day, which figured to be roughly thirty-six drinks. Appalled, the doctor asked how he then felt each morning. Frank said, "I don't know. I'm never up in the morning and I'm not sure you're the doctor for me."

The doctor died not long afterward, which in no small way always tickled the hubris of a certain impossible patient.

"I'm for anything that gets you through the night, be it prayer, tranquilizers, or a bottle of Jack Daniel's."

When men were men, where did they hang out after hours?

"In the early days when I palled around with Jackie Gleason, we used to go to Toots Shor's saloon. Between the two of us, we hardly ever had any bread. If we had a job (and in those days, that wasn't often), we'd meet at Tootsie's bar after — and sometimes before — work. It was a jumping kind of place. Toots Shor's was our clubhouse and Toots was a dear friend. He said we brought no class to his joint and we always had a lengthy tab. He complained that whenever we did have money, we blew it uptown at the Stork Club — which was true."

It was all about the guy who ran the joint: To Toots, they were both crumb-bums. Toots did not mince words. He was that way — a big, fat palooka whose gruff exterior could not quite mask a sentimental cream puff underneath. Said Gleason, "He'd call everybody crumb-bums — or stew-bums if you were drinking, which, of course, we were — then he'd pretend to ignore you in his restaurant. But later he'd come over and sit with you. I told him one time that the best thing you could say for his food was that it was warm. But it was where all the good guys went."

So there they went, to East Fifty-first Street around the corner from "21," Sinatra and Gleason, not quite into their thirties, on epic benders to which they signed tabs with empty promises. Because Toots was the softest touch for a handout, they would torment him mercilessly: Frank would watch Gleason routinely borrow three hundred bucks from Toots, then throw the crisp bills on the bar and announce, "Drinks for the house!" And Frank would fall to the floor, holding his sides. (When most amused, he always fell down laughing.)

Once, Gleason sponged five hundred dollars off Toots to hire a limo that would take him and Frank no farther than a few doors down Fifty-first Street to a jazz club where a one-armed trumpet player named Wingy Manone was playing. The limo, Frank recalled, "probably cost all of twenty bucks in those days. The rest of the money Gleason kept tossing at Wingy — in hundred-dollar bills — to play 'That's a Plenty' over and over again. When Toots saw that limousine only going less than one hundred feet, he blew his top. He barred both of us from his saloon for a month — but we ignored the ban."

SALOON STORY, MID-FORTIES: *His Finest Moment at Toots Shor's.* "I was sitting around one evening about seven, eight o'clock at the Waldorf-Astoria, where I was doing midnight shows, and Toots Shor called me. He said, 'Dago, get over here! I want you to meet a couple of friends of mine.' I said, 'Are you buying?' He said, 'When don't I buy? You bums haven't picked up a check in fifteen years in this joint!' So I went over there and he said, 'Just wait right here at the bar — let's have a drink.' About fifteen minutes later, in comes Mr. Crosby, who had just gotten back from Europe. We had been friends for years, so we had a little touch.

"Another person comes in — Jack

25

Dempsey, the famous boxer. I looked at Toots and said, 'This is a frame-up!' He said, 'Of course it is. I invited all you bums to come and have dinner with me tonight.' I said, 'It's a hell of a way to get us down here!'

"But that wasn't enough. Now Babe Ruth walks in the room! When Babe Ruth walked in, I damned near wet my pants. Because I'd never met him before. I knew Dempsey and certainly Bing — but Ruth! Toots started to lead us to a table. As you went from the bar into the restaurant area, they had what were called 'celebrity tables' at the left and the right, where you were usually seated. But this time, he didn't do that. He walked us all the way back into the main room near the fireplace, where there was a huge table.

"As we walked through the room, everyone in the entire place stood up and applauded. I turned to Bing and he had tears in his eyes. I said, 'Oh, you're such a *strong* man!' He said, 'Don't tell it to me. Look in the mirror at yourself, you bum!' All of us were so shaken by what had happened to us. I mean, they just stood and cheered and hollered because the four of us walked into the room at the same time. It's something I will never, never, never forget for as long as I breathe."

What makes for a perfect after-hours joint?

"A good piano player, good conversation, and people who like to stay up late. And some food helps. Jilly's had Howie at his joint, one of the best Chinese cooks in the city. It was a great hangout."

When a man enters his favorite place and the place is Jilly's, which is no more, but was, at Fifty-second and Eighth Avenue, and the year is, say, 1964, and the time is two A.M., and the man is at his peak of power, which is power like no man has known, because he is Sinatra, this is what happens:

His guys flank him, per custom, as he steps inside, and now he is bathed in the dusky light cast by orange flame lamps above the bar. He stops at the hat check and pats the girl on her cheek, smiles and says, "Hiya, sweetheart!" She melts a little. A path is cleared along the narrow bar so that he can move forward, move briskly, toward the back, the very back room, whose portal is roped off, like a red velvet Mason-

27

Dixon, to delineate where his sanctuary begins. Bobby Cole is at the piano, on top of which is propped a framed picture of Sinatra, who winks at Bobby as he approaches. Lifting back the velvet rope is Mike, the Irish maitre d', in gleaming tuxedo, whom Frank likes to call Miguel, whom he wraps his arms around, whose cheek he kisses, then teases in a foolish Irish brogue, forbidding him to march in the Columbus Day parade, where Irishmen are unwelcome. This is their routine.

Jilly has his table ready, the long booth to the left, against the back wall, beyond the piano, near the air-conditioner and the service door and the TV set. And his chair is ready, too; it is a worn imitation-leather high-backed armchair, which is put away when he is gone and brought back out whenever he returns. Jilly Rizzo, whom Frank loves, is a large slab of a man with a glass eye, thus a wavering gaze, who speaks in muddled street parlance. Such as: "When he comes in my room, it's like a terrific thrill for me which I am a guy that has seen a lot." Damon Runyon could have invented him. Frank first spotted Jilly sitting ringside at the Copa, during a performance in the fifties. "Who's that guy with the bad eye in the front row?" he asked afterward.

They met and became instant friends.

Before taking his chair, Frank will pop through the service doors where he hollers a greeting to diminutive cook Howard Eng, or Howie, whose chicken chow mein he adores and whose dialect he lampoons. Because the kitchen is in the basement, he yells down through the dumbwaiter tube: "Futt you, Hohrrie!" To which Howie responds, "Futt you, too, Flahnk!" ("All the time, same thing," says Howie, who, years later, would wear a gold wristwatch inscribed, "Futt you, Love, Francis.")

Jilly's inimitable version of this: "When Frank comes here, he always goes down in the kitchen and he talks to the Chink chef. He always kids around, talkin' that Chinese crap, *'Ah so, ah so,'* you know what I mean? And the chef, he's always giggling, so they kid around. Then Frank asks him if he's got his chicken chow mein ready, and the chef he says, 'Two minute! Two minute!' He eats the entire order of chow mein with soft noodles, which this is a man who isn't a big dinner eater, so it's a terrific kick for me. I couldn't even eat that much."

Frank calls his waiter Eyeglasses, whose actual name is Joe and who wears a red jacket and spectacles. Eyeglasses, and only Eyeglasses, brings the drinks and the chow mein, which Frank orders for everyone at his table, whose number might include Jill St. John or Tony Bennett or Judy Garland or his ex-wife Nancy or Dean Martin or Sammy Davis Jr. or his daughter Nancy or whichever friends of his are in town. From his special chair, he considers the considerable action in the room and over at the long dark bar — "He sorts of likes to stare into a room," is how Jilly put it. Frank, taking stock on one such night: "Jesus, there's about forty-three indictments right at the bar!" His presence ignites this room; people get louder, more gregarious, perhaps to earn validation in his eyes. "Five minutes after he's in the place, forget it — the place is New Year's Eve," Irish Mike would tell *Esquire*. And the civilians will creep to the rope and peer back toward him and sometimes he will wave a few through and shake their hands and smile, then go back to his conversation, telling the latest jokes that he has heard.

One such night, while holding court, he was caught in action by CBS News: He wore a dark suit and never loosened his tie or undid a button, which he would not ever deign to do in public. A dozen or so people hung on his words, which were quite animated, and he laughed a great deal and continually rose from his chair to act out stories and to greet friends. But the cameras were an unprecedented breach of security; photography was ill-advised on the premises. "If you were smart, you never took a picture inside Jilly's," one Sinatra intimate recalls. "Not a good idea. You had to respect privacy. That club had the biggest cross-section of people you could ever imagine. You could have Van Cliburn and Robert Merrill at one table; a senator and a judge and a congressman at another table; the heart surgeon Dr. Michael DeBakey at another; and over in the corner you'd have twenty years of good behavior. And then across from them there'd be three working girls."

He was probably the reason that any of them came there. If it was Frank's place, it was the place to be, which he knew. And he, too, would go there to be — to just be and relax. According to whim, he got there when he got there, no matter the time. One night, the lore goes, he was not in a happy mood when he arrived, at midnight, and the room felt his tenseness. So there was a hush as he strode into the back, where Johnny Carson happened to be sitting with Ed McMahon at a nearby table. Carson, who found amusement in the reverential silence, looked at Sinatra, then at his watch, and said, "Frank, I told you *twelve-thirty!*" At which point — and the story varies here — either Frank fell down laughing or Ed grabbed Johnny and hustled him out into the safety of the night.

THE PLACES HE WENT: By the eighties, Jilly's was gone, because Jilly had gone west, to Palm Springs, to be near Frank, and there he opened Jilly's West, with Frank's help; then he closed that, too. (For a while, there was also a Jilly's South, in Miami, just so Frank would have somewhere to go after playing the Fontainebleau or the Eden Roc.) But there would be hangouts in every city, where his picture would grace walls, anointing joints with an eight-by-ten benediction, the conferring of which thrilled him like a kid. "He loved having his picture on that wall," says his friend Jack McHugh, who owned a Chicago boîte called the Four Torches. "He'd come in and say, 'Where's my picture? Why isn't that picture bigger?' He loved doing that. He wanted everyone to know that was a hangout for him."

Whatever the place, he refused to be isolated from action or sequestered in a walled-off nook. "He doesn't want to go sit in an empty room," said Hank Cattaneo, of the final road nights. "It doesn't bother him

"Me and My Shadow"

having a crowd around. He loves people."
The only implicit understanding was that
the place let him stay well past closing time,
for no liquor license curfew could contain
him. Few did not oblige most happily.
(Their gratuities would inevitably be epic.)
And so, after Jilly's in New York was shut-
tered, there would be PATSY'S and "21"
and, at the Waldorf-Astoria, where he kept
an apartment, a certain spot he liked to call
Sir Herpes, because of the alleged late-night
prostitute clientele. (In that vein, another famous bar in Vegas became known in his
circle as the Gonorrhea Bar.) In San Francisco, there were the old EL MATADOR and
BLUE FOX and the NEW ORLEANS ROOM
at the Fairmont Hotel. In Philly, there were

BOOKBINDERS and RALPH'S and PALUM-BO'S. In Chicago, there were always the PUMP ROOM, at his beloved Ambassador East Hotel, and the rib joint TWIN ANCHORS, then later GIBSONS, across the street from which some of his old road *paisans* opened, as an homage, JILLY'S, whose cocktail napkins bear the declaration *My Favorite Bistro — Frank Sinatra*. In Los Angeles, after ROMANOFF'S and VILLA CAPRI and his own PUCCINI'S, even after CHASEN'S and BISTRO GARDENS, there would be NICKY BLAIR'S and MATTEO'S and LA DOLCE VITA. After which, in recent years, he would repair to the PENINSULA HOTEL bar, to smoke and drink, piano-side.

"Wherever we went after dinner would have to include a piano player and a bar," Shirley MacLaine wrote in a memoir, recalling a concert tour they shared. "Frank knew piano bars that no one else knew." The tinkling and the plinking always caressed and soothed his psyche, carried him away, reminding him of forgotten tunes and of old adventures. Even after he had sung hours earlier for thousands of people, he liked nothing more than to sing again, very quietly, for a few. This was ballad time. He did it often with Bobby Cole at Jilly's — these were magnificent nights — sitting

Ballad time (left to right)*: Jimmy Van Heusen, Sammy Cahn, and FS*

there, elbow on the piano, drink in hand, just vocalizing to make himself feel better. He even did it on the night of his eightieth-birthday spectacular, after he had sat through three grueling hours of goddamned musical tributes to him at the Shrine Auditorium in Los Angeles. He never really cared for that adulatory jazz; it made him feel old and left out, two things whose meanings he could not comprehend. Always, he would much rather be doing the singing.

So he did. When he got the hell out of the Shrine, his group took over a back room at the Four Seasons Hotel restaurant, which was dead at that hour. The hotel manager placed a panicked phone call to the regular lounge pianist, woke him up, and got him back there — almost an hour after the Sinatras and their friends had arrived. Frank was getting crankier by the minute. "Where the hell have *you* been?" he barked when Dana Bronson finally slipped behind the piano. But the music made everything all right, as it will. And there he stood, with Steve Lawrence on the opposite side of the piano, working his way through the old tunes again, for an intimate cluster accustomed to such scenes — Eydie Gorme, Gregory and Veronique Peck, Robert Wagner and Jill St. John, Tony Bennett. Occasionally, one of Frank's guys would whisper titles into Bronson's ear, like "My Funny Valentine" and "Imagination" and "Laura," songs that always pleased the boss.

"He was more talkin' 'em than singin' 'em," Bronson would say. "At one point, I was playing 'Night and Day,' and he turned to me and said, 'Don't you know the opening verse?' I told him I actually didn't, and he said, 'How long have you been playin' piano?' I kind of vamped it for him, but it was apparent that music is very important to him. He had a story to tell about every song I played. Like: 'I recorded that in 1938 in Newark, New Jersey, and the trumpet player forgot to wear socks that day.' When I played 'Penthouse Serenade,' an old song from the thirties, he just stopped cold and said, *'I love this fuckin' song!'* I figured he liked me when he cursed in front of me."

As ever, his mood was much improved when he left, very late.

Ring-a-Ding-Ding!

"*You've gotta love livin', baby! Because dyin' is a pain in the ass!*"

"*I'm not one of those complicated, mixed-up cats. I'm not lookin' for the secret to life or the answer to life. I just go on from day to day, takin' what comes.*"

"*Man, I'm buoyant. I feel about eight feet tall.*"

Come on, George. LOOSEN UP. SWING, MAN. *Dust off those gossamer wings and fly yourself to* THE MOON OF YOUR CHOICE *and be grateful to carry the baggage we've all had to carry since those* LEAN NIGHTS *of sleeping on buses and helping the driver unload the instruments.*

And no more of that talk about "the tragedy of fame." The tragedy of fame is when no one shows up and YOU'RE SINGING TO THE CLEANING LADY *in some empty joint that hasn't seen a paying customer* SINCE ST. SWITHIN'S DAY. *And you're nowhere near that; you're the top dog on* THE TOP RUNG OF A TALL LADDER *called Stardom, which in Latin means thanks-to-the-fans who were there when it was lonely.*

Talent must not be wasted. Those who have talent — and you obviously do or Calendar's *cover article would have been about Rudy Vallee — those who have talent* MUST HUG IT, *embrace it, nurture it and share it,* LEST IT BE TAKEN AWAY *from you as fast as it was loaned to you.*

TRUST ME. I'VE BEEN THERE.

— LETTER TO THE *Los Angeles Times,* SEPTEMBER 16, 1990, IN RESPONSE TO AN ARTICLE ABOUT "RELUCTANT" POP STAR GEORGE MICHAEL

How does one live large?

"You just keep moving."

$\mathscr{M}$oss must never grow. "You only live once — and the way I live, once is enough," he said upon turning fifty. "I look upon this as the halfway mark," he also said. He had plans to swing forever more. Like mercury, he would not be pinned down, would never sit tight. He was all about *action.* "Let's keep it moving please, because if it bogs down, it's *deadly,*" he would tell his conductors in recording studios. But that was his way. When held in place, his physical presence seemed to radiate geothermally. Thus he was *felt* in a room before he was ever seen. "You feel an *impact,* even when he doesn't do or say anything," Steve Lawrence would attest. Producer Stanley Kramer once said, "When Sinatra walks into a room, tension walks in beside him." Atmosphere crackled; other men were infected, absorbed his power, got louder, bigger.

43

A nucleus among men, *his* men especially, he lent out the hubris, covered every ass, cleared the forest, rigged the tempo, made the rules. His daughter Nancy interprets the phenomenon: "He believes you must play it big, wide, expansively — the more open you are, the more you take in, your dimensions deepen, you grow, you become more what you are — bigger, richer." Result: "He is better than anybody else, or at least they think he is, and he has to live up to it."

And so he lived, and so they took his lead. They followed, man and woman alike. Tom Dreesen gives illustration: "They were all in Las Vegas shooting *Ocean's Eleven*, and one morning the actor Norman Fell woke up and looked outside of his hotel window. He saw Dean and Sammy and Peter Lawford running past the pool, running *fast*. So he stuck his head out and yelled, 'Hey, where are you guys going?' And Sammy said, '*Frank's up!*' So the day begins. You have to understand that when you are with Frank Sinatra, it's his world and you are living in it. When Frank says we're going, we go; when he says we're sitting, we sit. If you revolve around his energy, you benefit. With Frank, you can never learn enough."

"LET'S START THE ACTION!" he would howl,

44

sounding the gun. Where the action wasn't he would not be. On movie sets, he could not bear inaction or self-indulgent directors. "I can't stay in one place for sixteen weeks," he told one. "I'll kill myself!" Frank Capra once said of him, "He bores easily. If directors keep him busy, he maintains an uneasy truce; for having started something, Sinatra's next goal is to finish it — but fast." (How Frank initiated one film negotiation with Capra, whom he called Cheech: "Cheech! Why don't you and I make *Hole in the Head* together? You do all the dirty work, while I smile and knock off all the broads.") Making *Some Came Running*, on location in Madison, Indiana, he seethed at the artistic futzing of director Vincente Minnelli. One night, he and Dean Martin and Shirley MacLaine waited endlessly on a carnival set, while Minnelli sized up a camera angle. Dissatisfied, the director decided not to shift his lens; rather, he declared, "Move the Ferris wheel!" Frank turned, leaped into a car, boarded his jet, and was back in Los Angeles hours later. Dean went with him.

WHENEVER BORED AT A PARTY OR A CLUB, he would say this: "I think it's going to rain." This was the signal to depart. He would rise and take a powder, his entourage in tow.

Then they would go seek fresh stimuli, on the loose, on the Strip, on the town, moving in a pack, like, well, never mind. He meant for no umbrage to be taken when he saw the rain coming, when the restlessness gripped him. It was biological: "I can't help it," he would tell Minnelli, not quite apologetically. "Nobody seems to be able to help me with it. I've got to go! I have to move!"

Few could stop him or would dare to try. He led a group into the showroom of the Sahara to watch Don Rickles perform. This was 1965. About an hour into the act, Frank stood up and yelled to the comic: "All right, c'mon, let's get this thing over with. I gotta go!" Rickles shot back: "Shad-dup and sit down! I've had to listen to you sing!" Frank: "Who do you think you're talking to?" Rickles: "Dick Haymes." Frank laughed, whereupon his group laughed, and they stayed. For a little while.

Explain the secret
language of
swagger.

"I once asked Jimmy Cagney
how he explained it. And he
said, 'Francis, always sprinkle
the goodies along the way. Be
as tough as you want, but always sprinkle the goodies here
and there. Because anything
they can laugh at, they can't
hate.' "

*H*e crept up behind Cagney on a movie
lot one day and mimicked the tiny master:
"Mmmmmm . . . you dirty rat." Cagney did
not flinch. "He never turned around," said
Frank. "He only said, 'Francis, that's the
worst imitation I've ever heard in my life.' "
Clearly, he needed to find his own style,
which of course he did. The Sinatra bra-
vado twinkled through baby blues. He exerted force through a grin, led with rhythm
and snap, swung cocksure. "I think that
that's kind of inbred," he once said, pon-
dering the way he swung, thus swaggered.
"I think you have or haven't got it. I'm
probably one of the fortunate people to

Language lessons

whom it was given. I never thought about it much." But he could not play the role of *il padrone* straight and somber, without breeze, for who would follow and where would the laughs be? So he mixed his menace with tonic. For instance, the sign on the front gate of his Coldwater Canyon bachelor pad in the fifties read: *If You Haven't Been Invited, You Better Have a Damned Good Reason for Ringing This Bell.* Later, at the Palm Springs compound, a gold plaque warned: *Never Mind the Dog — Beware of the Owner.*

Parlance was his muscle and signature. He spoke in a language of his own devising, a shorthand cool that bristled and baffled and was readily contagious. From the Sammy Davis Jr. memoir, *Why Me?*: "A young cat with two wild-looking chicks walked by and Frank raised his eyebrows. *'Cuff links.'* " This was the lingo of ring-a-ding-ding and, like any secret code, it was beloved by boys and anathema to girls. After spending time in his midst, one woman reporter said, "For years I tried to get an exclusive interview — and when I got one, I couldn't understand a word he said." A Vegas lounge arm-piece to the Pack confessed: "They might just as well have been talking Chinese."

Language pupil Sophia Loren

Some pupils were more awkward than others. After taking English lessons from Sinatra, while making *The Pride and the Passion*, young Sophia Loren could be heard peppering casual conversation with the phrases: "How's your cock?" and "It was a fucking gas!" (He told her that *cock* and *fucking* were innocent endearments, to be employed freely and often. Of Loren, incidentally, Frank liked to say, "She's the mostest!") Noel Coward, who occasionally moved amid the Sinatra group, was spotted at one of Frank's performances happily crowing: "It's a gas! It's a gas!" Even bona fide pally Peter Lawford tended to abuse the privileged argot: "Like, we were getting off the boat the other day in Le Havre," he told an interviewer, "and this French dame comes up to me and says, *'Etes-vous un Rat?'* She's asking me, am I a Rat? I don't dig. Then I dig. She's asking me about the Rat Pack, you dig? But there's no word in French for Rat Pack, you dig?"

NAVIGATIONAL TIPS FOR THE UNINITIATED: "A GAS IS A GOOD SITUATION," the Leader once translated for Art Buchwald, in an unprecedented act of decoding. "An evening can be a wonderful gas. Or you can have a gas of a weekend." Therefore, a GASSER was one who instilled such delight: "Applies to a person. He's a big-leaguer, the best. He can hit the ball right out of the park." (More BROADS were gassers than were guys, understandably so. Should a gasser do something wonderful, she would be rewarded with the exclamation, CRAZY! or maybe COO-COO! When pleased by a pally, meanwhile, Frank showed approval by remarking, YOU CRAZY BASTARD!) On the other hand, a BUNTER would be "the opposite of a gasser . . . a NOWHERE. He can never get to first base." Likewise, there was HARVEY: "A square. Harvey, or Harv, is the typical tourist who goes into a French restaurant and says, 'What's ready?' " CLYDE was no better, for *clydes* were DULLSVILLE personified, were instructed to SCRAMSVILLE, lest they render an evening ENDSVILLE. Otherwise, *clyde* was an all-purpose noun employed when words, wit, or memory failed. Explained Frank: "If I want someone to pass the salt, I say, 'Pass the clyde.' 'I don't like her clyde,' might mean,

'I don't like her voice.' 'I have to go to the clyde' could mean 'I have to go to the party.' "

If said party cooked, which is to say, was MOTHERY, which is to say, was wild and wicked, then all present would bear witness to a RING-A-DING-DING time, after which couples might pair off to make a LITTLE HEY-HEY. Unless a FINK had infiltrated the scene to queer the odds. "A *fink* is a loser," said Frank. "*Fink* comes from a strike-breaker named Fink who killed his friend during a strike. So to me a fink is a guy who would kill his own friends." (Dead

friends, by the way, bought the BIG CASINO in the sky.) Further: "If a guy comes into a room with a broad and someone asks about his wife, the guy will say, 'GOOD NIGHT, ALL,' which means, 'DROP IT, CHARLEY.' " Charley, in that case, would be a fink, or CRUMB. Thus the phrase LET'S LOSE CHAR-

LEY. But then every pally was affectionately called Charley at one point or another, male or female, and also SAM, but mostly Charley. (Lawford was Charley the Seal, for his nicotine cough, or Charley Pentagon or Charley Washington, because he married a Kennedy. Sometimes Frank simply called him Brother-in-Lawford.) Then again, a CHICK might easily FRACTURE, or amuse, or devastate, a man who got a load of her nice set of CHARLEYS. If that man was Sinatra, and a date was made, then he would be ALL LOCKED UP for that night, so he would bid his boys adieu, telling them, "TA-TA."

STANDARD SINATRA GREETING: "HOW'S YOUR BIRD?"

His concern was anatomical. As always, there were variations:

"How's your Bell and Howell?"

"How's your Foster, Charley?"

"How's your cornpone, baby?"

But BIRD was the word that thrilled him most, and he would sneak it into any context whenever possible. Onstage, he would sing, "She loves the free, fresh clyde in her bird" or "I've got you under my bird" or "Just say the words and we'll beat our birds down to Acapulco Bay." After he nearly drowned in Hawaii in 1964, his only public acknowledgment was, "Oh, I just got a little water on my bird, that's all." To inquire about a man's romantic conquests, he'd say, "Did you grow any orchids in your bird this weekend?" Of any bumbler, he'd say, "He does have a way of stepping on his bird." Signing a photograph of himself wielding a Jack Daniel's bottle, he wrote for a friend: "Drink, Dickie! It's good for your bird."

But he did not reserve the term for men only. Once, at the El Matador in San Francisco, he obliged a prim Englishwoman who approached him for an autograph, then asked after her bird. "I — I don't have a bird," she replied, confused. "Oh, lady," he said, "then you're in *deep* trouble!" She pinkened with embarrassment, which he instantly regretted. So he seated her at his table and gave her champagne and charmed away the fluster. Birds, after all, do have their place.

Swagger Story, Early Seventies:

Chops were flexed whenever he perceived that a little guy was getting the rub. One night, he sat in the kitchen of Nicky Blair's on Sunset Boulevard, playing poker with Burt Reynolds, Jilly Rizzo, and the usual fellas. A Mexican busboy named Hector rushed by and dropped a tray of glasses, shattering them everywhere. Nicky Blair stormed in and fired the kid on the spot. Frank looked up and said, "Just a minute, Nicky. How much do those glasses cost?"

"I don't know, Mr. S. Ten, twenty dollars apiece, why?"

Frank gave a signal to one of his guys, who pulled out a wad of cash and peeled off forty-five C-notes, then handed them over to Nicky.

"Bring me forty-five hundred dollars' worth of glasses," Frank told him.

The restaurateur shrugged. Hundreds of glasses were bustled forth and placed at Sinatra's feet. Next, Frank called over the fired busboy.

"Hector, do you see all these glasses?" he said.

"*Si.*"

"Good. Now break 'em."

Which he did, until there were no more. Then Frank addressed Nicky: "Every time I come in here I want to see Hector working for you. Understand what I'm saying?"

Said Nicky, beaming, "I always loved Hector!"

What is the best thing to do with money?

"You gotta spend it. Move it around."

Tightwads, he disdained. Occasionally, while drinking, he amused himself by putting together his El Cheapo All-Time All-Star baseball team. Rudy Vallee was always pitcher. Even friends like Cary Grant and Bob Hope and Fred MacMurray usually made the lineup. Of one who was parsimonious, he would say, quoting comedian Joe E. Lewis, "He has an impediment in his reach." This, of course, was never his problem. Don Rickles said of him, "He gets up in the morning and God throws money on him." To which Frank retorted, "And I throw it back."

Very long ago, he offhandedly remarked, "I've always wanted to carry a million dollars in my pocket." It was not a pipe dream. When he carried money at all, rarely did he carry anything less than hundred-dollar bills, crisp and new, usually twenty of them, often more, folded into his gold, pointed money clip. Coins never jangled in his pockets; he especially loathed pennies. "He hated them even when he was a kid," says Nancy Jr. "He used to throw them away." Such caprice only magnified with age — exponentially so, once Las Vegas became his fiefdom. Quoth vibraphonist bandleader Red Norvo, in 1960: "I've seen him go up to the baccarat table with ten thousand

dollars, sit down, put the bundle on the table, ride it up to thirty thousand, lose it, and walk away with a shrug." (He loved baccarat because it was fast, it *moved;* another night he lost fifty thousand, *fast,* and again he shrugged.)

When he got killed at blackjack — he always sat at the third base position — he never blinked, just gave a nod and said, "Good dealer," then strode off, all nonchalance.

Fearless men cannot fear ruin: And so he would sniff and say, "Money doesn't interest me." He refused to worry about it, ever. When he had none, he spent as though he did; when he became rich, he spent as though there was no end to it. By the time he turned thirty, he had given away fifty thousand dollars' worth of gold cigarette lighters. If haberdashers were summoned to spread swank bounty before him, he would call in his nearest lieutenants and decree, "Help yourself, fellas. I'm gifting today." He bestowed shiny tokens at every turn — watches, cuff links, pinkie rings, cars. Soon, like contagion, all Pack members were giving each other, and everybody else, engraved mementos. "I wanted to be like him so bad," said Sammy, who — big-hearted bum that he was — perhaps overly dedicated himself to the goal. Classic Sam story: Blowing his bread Sinatra-style had caught up with him and he suddenly found himself in dire straits. So he was sent to a new accountant, who sat him down and lowered the boom. He had to stop spending or he'd have less than nothing. Sammy listened patiently, promised to adhere to a crunched budget, then left. The next day, the accountant received a gold Cartier cigarette case with the inscription: *Thanks for the advice. Sammy.*

Frank, however, could not comprehend even the suggestion of such restraint. Life was his indulgence: He learned of the birth of his first grandchild while dining out in New York with a friend. To celebrate, he immediately told the waiter to bring him thirty thousand clams. "You can't do that," his friend said, foolishly. "Yes, I can," he blurted. "I'm a grandfather and I want thirty thousand clams. In bowls, a hundred at a time!" (They stopped eating after the first few hundred.) In the mid-sixties, out of the blue, he ordered his lawyer to buy an office building in Los Angeles. "But it's not for sale," the lawyer told him. "I want it," said Frank. "Why?" asked the lawyer. "They won't let me land my helicopter on top," he explained.

By that time, Sinatra owned three private jets, the first of which — christened *El Dago* — he acquired in 1959, back when entertainers didn't think about buying planes. Onstage, he sung about it, most defiantly: "When I'm up there wingin', I'm really ring-a-ding-dingin' . . . ." Thusly equipped, he flew friends everywhere, paid for everything, doled out mad money to any women along for the ride. (In Vegas or Monte Carlo, ladies received bags of casino chips; whenever luck failed any of them, he covered all markers.) If airlifted to the Palm Springs compound, they were pampered fully and plied with booze never-ending. His house guests affectionately called him the Innkeeper, so zealous and thorough was his hospitality. In each of the plush guest bungalows, he *personally* stocked medicine cabinets with everything from eye pads to toothpaste to tampons. Rosalind Russell described him as "a knitter-together of people, a constant plate-filler and glass-replenisher." Gifts arrived on breakfast trays each morning. When he hosted a weekend for **Jack Benny's eightieth birthday**, Benny's

The well-stocked El Dago

The Innkeeper tosses a birthday bash for Edward G. Robinson

wife, Mary Livingstone, found a Van Cleef and Arpels bracelet the first morning, a Cartier watch the next. On the third morning, when the tray came with merely food, she left a note: "What happened, Frank? This morning . . . nothing?"

"Every meal was a party," says the writer Garson Kanin, who visited often with his wife, Ruth Gordon. One day Frank promised a Mexican dinner, so he flew everyone to Acapulco to consume it. Another day, lunching at the Tamarisk Golf Club, he heard Ruth Gordon ordering a slice of raw onion for her hamburger. Frank said, "The onion they have here is no good. You gotta have Maui onions if you're gonna have a hamburger." The actress had never heard of the Polynesian produce. "Oh, for cryin' out loud!" said Frank, walking off. Two bushels of Maui onions were flown in from Hawaii the next day.

"We were guests, true," says Kanin, "but looking back, it seems that we were all actors in a play that was full of charm and grace written, cast, and directed by Frank."

Tipping as art form: the final word

> "Just duke 'em, for
> Chrissakes!"

 In the realm of gratuities, his legend towers. He was unrivaled, for he insisted that it be so. True lore: Restaurant parking attendant brings around Frank's Dual Ghia, Frank asks him what his biggest tip ever was, kid says a hundred bucks, Frank slips him two hundred, then asks who it was that gave him the hundred. "You did, sir, last week."

That was nothing. "Whoever he tipped

could go buy a mansion in Paris," says Don Rickles, who witnessed his palm-greasing the world over. But one had to be vigilant to observe such transactions. It was a discreet business, never executed with flourish. "He never showed off," says Tom Dreesen. "He would never flash a bill." Unless he was alone, he rarely did the dole himself, preferring not to touch the currency. In the old days at Toots Shor's, Toots took pleasure in reaching into Frank's pocket to extract bills, which he mirthfully distributed to his staff. Frank said nothing, just watched with amusement.

He called it *duking* and he duked almost always in C-notes. The phrase is lifted from the saloons of Tin Pan Alley, wherein if a crumb "dipped his duke in the tambourine," he was in fact skimming from the cash register, grabbing extra bread on the sly. Sinatra's tambourine overflowed for dukes everywhere, ever sly.

He never duked his way into any joint, did it only on the way out. But then, if you are he, your table always awaits.

The bills were folded three times into small squares, so as to be subtly passed in a handshake. The men of Sinatra carried wads of hundreds to peel on his behalf, at his whim. Songwriter Jimmy Van Heusen, whose real name was Chester Babcock, whom Frank called Chester Babcock, often held the cash in the fifties. Whenever Frank gave him the sign of the cross, Chester had to duke at least one hundred fifty dollars. Jilly never carried less than two grand. What with inflation, and the Leader's ever-growing largesse, the men who succeeded him toted even more. Hank Cattaneo says, "He'd always say, sotto voce, 'Duke this guy a hundred!' And then two minutes later: 'Did you duke him a hundred?' I'd say yeah. 'Well, duke him again!' He'd get a crowd of waiters and waitresses real quick. It wasn't unusual for us to end up giving one or two girls five hundred dollars apiece in an evening, then do it all over again the next night. I'd say, 'Frank, enough, *enough!*' But, you know, he doesn't understand *enough.*"

Pallies

Frank Sinatra's calling
And it means tonight
* we're balling*
All the way . . .
Many fears soon plague us:
Is it Palm Springs,
* is it Vegas?*
Who can say?
Thank God there's just
* one Sinatra*
With two Franks,
* it wouldn't play.*
So drink up to the Rat Pack
And be proud that you're
* with that Pack*
All the way,
* all the way . . .*

— SUNG TO FS ON HIS BIRTHDAY,
1957, BY SAMMY CAHN

PETER (Reading newspaper): *Listen to this one: "The quintet of Sinatra, Martin, Davis, Lawford, and Bishop moved into Las Vegas in the form of an attack force with Sinatra as the nominal leader of their clan."*
FRANK: *I don't want to be the Leader. One of you guys be the Leader.*
PETER: *Sorry, Frank, but it says here you're the Leader.*
SAMMY: *Hold it! I wanta go on record that I ain't belongin' to nothing that's called a clan.*
DEAN: *I don't know, pally* (nods at Frank). *You'd better discuss that with the Leader.*

— IN THE SANDS HOTEL STEAM ROOM,
JANUARY 28, 1960

I would simply like to say that all the fun that happens here onstage happens offstage as well. It's constantly a Thing. And Frank, being the Leader, is thinking all the time. You know, making up little games to play, like Let's Punch Someone Out. Things like that . . .

— SAM IN THE SANDS HOTEL
COPA ROOM, 1963

How do you know when you've found a friend for life?

"You bypass the acquaintanceship stage immediately. Either your currents are different and the chemistry isn't there or else you're hooked and you're a friend immediately — and, in most cases, permanently."

He was the friend everyone wanted. Princes and presidents, goddesses and godfathers, moguls and matzohs, they all sidled forth in hopes of currying his favor. He made more of anyone, conferred status and safety that mere fortune could not provide. Sam called him the Umbrella. His loyalty was impervious, his gestures of kindness were ferocious. "You can have my last drop of blood," he would tell those who mattered, those he believed would do the same for him. An only child forever, he played Big Brother in so many lives: "Oh, I just wish someone would try to hurt you so I

71

could kill them for you," he'd say, again and again, to a naive young Shirley Mac-Laine. In 1947 he put his arm around little Sam at New York's Capitol Theater when they worked together for the first time, and told him, "Anything I can ever do for you — you've got yourself a friend for life." Then he added, as ever, "And remember — if anybody hits you, let me know." Dean Martin once said, "Frank and I are broth-ers, right? We cut the top of our thumbs and became blood brothers. He wanted to cut the wrist. I said, 'What, are you *crazy*? No, *here's* good enough.'"

DEAN WAS HIS BALANCE, the man he could not be, but wished he was. By origins *italiano*, they were opposites: Dean was Abruzzese, stoic in nature; Frank was Sicilian, passionate by birthright. Dean was a complex but fluffy nimbus rolling gently across the azure; Frank was a storm cloud, pouring love (or hate or joy), always in torrents. "Frank takes things seriously; I don't," said Dag, as Sinatra affectionately called him. ("The only one who can call me Dago is Frank," he once explained. "I call him Dago, too. With anybody else, there's a fight.") In a rare moment of introspection, Frank said: "I'm too much of a volatile man. I admire someone who can walk away after being needled, quietly ignoring the whole thing." He was thinking of Dag at the time. Once, they had gone to play the Crosby Open at Pebble Beach, arrived at the hotel after midnight, and found that room service had shut down. Frank got the manager on the phone, hollered, ordered him up to the room, and punches flew, while Dean sat watching television. "Hey," said Dean finally, "can you guys fight a little to the left. I'm having trouble seeing the picture."

Whereas other men leaped at the Leader's whim, Dean stood his ground, sauntered over at best. "Sure, I'd go where Frank goes," he once said, shrugging, but he never followed blindly, was the only one who ever asked Sinatra, "Why?" For this, he was respected, beloved, and considered in manner unspoken the Pack's second-in-command. He shot straight, was always funniest. At Sam "Momo" Giancana's Villa Venice, the suburban Chicago mob joint where they were summoned to perform in 1962, it was Dean who told Frank and Sam, "Hold down the noise! There's a gangster sleeping upstairs." He was fearless, like Frank, whom he did not know well before they made *Some Came Running* four years earlier. Dean got that part — of Bama, the boozy gambler pally — by accosting Frank at a party, addressing him thusly: "You bum!" Said Frank: "What have I done now?" Dean: "You're hunting a guy who smokes, drinks, and can talk real Southern? You're looking at him." Frank, after a long stare: "What do you know! You're right." The year after they acted together onscreen, they began to act up together onstage, for the first time, at the Sands (January 28, 1959), fusing the core of all clansmanship to come.

"WE AIN'T FIGURED OUT OURSELVES what the hell we do up here," stated the Leader, stalking the stage. "But it's fun, baby." Las Vegas, January 1960: He had called forth comrades he liked, whose talents he enjoyed, whose birds he could inquire after, and thrown them together, en masse, to play ex-members of the 82nd Airborne out to rob five casinos on New Year's Eve. This was *Ocean's Eleven* — the celluloid apotheosis of ring-a-ding-ding. Shooting by day, they cut loose at night, assuaging boredom by becoming the Rat Pack, as the press would call them. "I hate that stupid phrase," said Frank. Naturally, he led all capering, in film and in life. Before they were the Rat Pack, which he claimed they never were, they were called THE CLAN: himself and Dag and Sam and Pete Lawford and Joey Bishop composing the quintessential membership. "I hate the name Clan," Frank also said. When they gathered onstage, he always preferred that their convocation be known as the Summit. But this mattered little, for they were, alas and forever, the Rat Pack, whose satellite Charleys included Little Sister MacLaine (Shirl), Tony Curtis (Boinie, as in Bernie), Jimmy Van Heusen (Chester), Steve Lawrence (Boy Singer), Kirk Douglas, Don Rickles, Robert Wagner, and whomever else Frank wished to see drunk.

Camelot came to the Sands that February. Pulling himself off the campaign trail for a breather, the young senator from Massachusetts — whose sister was Lawford's wife — became known as Chicky-Baby, when addressed by the Leader. As with any politician, he knew Sinatra's endorsement translated to fund-raising dough ad infinitum. If Frank sang for him, his campaign coffers would brim. Meanwhile, Frank, who basked in power all his own, loved the idea of being near potential White House power. "Don't forget I've got Lawford, and remember who Lawford's got!" he would crow. (To show unabashed support, he momentarily renamed his merry cabal the Jack Pack.) John Fitzgerald Kennedy, who knew well how to recreate, thusly partook of the ongoing mothery gas. He watched ribald Clan meetings unfold onstage and afterward repaired to party suites to meet registered young female voters of Frank's acquaintance.

He also found welcome in the Sands steam room, which was the unofficial Summit clubhouse, where the boys met daily at five to clear the mucus of the previous night and plot ahead. There they spoke in colorful language, ate hot dogs and pizza, blew cherry bombs, threw cream pies at each other, and wore white monogrammed robes — except Sam, whose white robe was switched for brown on mirthful occasion. Across the back of his robe was SMOKEY; Frank's had FAS; Dean's had DAG. Joey,

whose robe bore his trademark catch-phrase SON OF A GUN, likes to recall, "When I first saw Frank nude in the steam room, he became my idol. When Sammy first saw me, I became *his* idol." Rickles gained induction by being tossed out into the pool area, naked, by Frank and Dean. "Frank thought that was funny," he says. "So I frightened a few small children, what did he care?" His robe said RHINO.

"You've got to go through the Bishop to get to the Pope," Joey would joke, somewhat exaggerating his rank of echelon. (The Leader was also called the Pope.) The Philly-born deadpan comic actually knew better: He later flirted with titling his never-written memoir *I Was a Mouse in the Rat Pack*. But, in truth, he was the architect of all Pack stagecraft, author of their trustiest "ad-libs." He hovered over the act, a needling moderator, concerned with pacing: "The casino bosses showed us how much money they lost if we went longer than an hour," he says. Frank called him the Speaker of the House. After Kennedy became President, Joe cooked up a bit where Lawford would wander through the audience wearing a busboy uniform, gather some dishes, and intone, "Imagine what I'd be doing if he didn't get elected!"

Bishop remembers: "For the first two or three times, he wasn't getting much of a laugh because he did not emphasize the word *didn't*. So I told him this and he said, 'Don't tell me how to deliver a line!' You know what Frank said to him? 'Deliver the line the way Joey's telling you or get the fuck out of the show!' " Lawford, who happily stayed on, mostly danced with Sam, flaunted his suave British charm, and acquiesced to Frank. (He named his daughter Victoria Frances, after Francis Albert.) Possessed of business savvy, he shared ownership with Sinatra in the Beverly Hills restaurant Puccini's and in *Ocean's Eleven*. It was Pete who first found the Vegas yarn, which was dreamed up by a Santa Monica gas station attendant. Once captured on film, the gas would flow eternally.

"We haven't seen much daylight since we've been here," Frank reported to audiences in the Copa Room. "Seen a lot of Jack Daniel's, but not much daylight." Their desert hijinks grabbed the imagination of the world, gave Las Vegas more romantic cachet than perhaps it ever deserved. They brought a better class of sin to Sin City. High rollers flocked to the Strip, always would whenever Frank and Dean performed in town — but this was Eventsville, and the

Sands was now mecca with a dress code. Money poured in. The boys ruled; they floated through the casino, Frank and Dean dealt blackjack, turned up the cards, and let all the pretty ladies win. (Nancy Jr. recalls: "If the dealer had twenty showing — that is, if Sinatra had twenty showing — and you had nineteen, he'd just keep hitting you until you got two aces or a deuce and then he'd take the extra cards away and say, 'Okay, you've got twenty-one!' And pay you with the house's money.") They did as they liked.

After their second show each night, they eventually moved to the lounge for gasoline and soft-shouldered scenery. "Everybody knew we'd all meet at the Sands lounge, okay?" says Tony Curtis. "We'd be sitting there getting looped and these *fabulous* girls would start coming in around two o'clock, girls who were getting off work in the chorus lines. They'd sit with us, under that dim lighting, with that music playing — I mean, it was too good! It wasn't about fucking as much as it was about *wooing*, you know? I'd look across four tables and there was Frank with two or more girls. But let me tell you, HE WASN'T A WOMANIZER — HE WAS WOMANIZED! What a great position to be in!" He adds, "You know, those were carefree, intelligent, and very stimulating days and nights."

Dean would come but never stay long. Only he could leave with impunity. He'd have one drink, two, tops, then lie to Frank and say, "I've got a girl in my room." It was never that big of a secret: "Do you know that I spill more than he drinks?" Frank would say. "That's an actuality." Dean's license plate read DRUNKY, but it was a sham. He mostly sipped and pretended. "I drink about one-tenth as much as I pretend to," he confessed. "I'll have a slug of a liquid in an old-fashioned glass that looks like scotch, but it's really apple juice." You could tell by his comic timing onstage, even more physically precise than that of the beloved monkey, former partner Jerry Lewis. "No one has ever seen me drunk," he once said. (That was not entirely true — Frank, of course, bore witness on occasion — but it was true for the most part.) When he did drink, it was J&B scotch, with three tablespoons of soda.

But in the lounge, his presence was brief and vaporous. He loved to sleep, then hit the morning links, nursing his glorious six handicap. Frank knew. "He likes golfball-thumpin' like I like humpin' — to each his own!" the Leader sang when the Friars roasted Dag. "They gave one another space," says Greg Garrison, Dean's long-time TV producer. Not that gauntlets weren't thrown: Once Frank gave a broad a grand to wait naked in Dean's bed. Dean gave her two grand to go back and tell Frank he was fabulous. Such was their love and mutual understanding.

Dean Story, Mid-Sixties

The Martins, Dean and Jeanne, were throwing themselves a black-tie anniversary party, a tented affair, in their backyard on Mountain Drive. A society orchestra was hired, people danced and cavorted and consumed a meal of many courses; white-coated bartenders poured gallons upon gallons of spirits. At just past eleven o'clock, police sirens pierced the air and halted the festivities. Alarmed, the hostess searched for her husband but could not find him. She went to Frank, who calmed her and said, "Don't worry about it — it's probably an accident out in front. I'll take care of it."

Frank strode out to find the Beverly Hills police planted on the lawn. "What's going on, fellas?" he asked. He was told: "Well, Mr. Sinatra, we got a call about a loud party. You're gonna have to tone it down — or maybe just break it up for the night." Since most of the neighbors were in attendance, Frank said, "Who the hell would call?"

"Um, I'm not really at liberty to say," the cop responded.

Frank gave him a look and said, "Hey! You're talkin' to *me* now."

The cop shuffled and said, "Well, to be totally honest with you, Mr. Sinatra, the call came from inside the house."

Frank shook his head, muttered under his breath, *"That son of a bitch."* Then said to the cops, "Okay, guys — thanks a lot."

He walked back into the house, climbed the stairs to Dean's bedroom, where Dag, in pajamas, lay in his bed, holding a putter, watching the eleven o'clock news. Glancing over at Frank: "Hey, pally."

Frank: "I'll give you *pally!* Did you call the cops on your own party?"

Dean, shrugging: "Hey, they ate, they drank. Let them go home. I gotta get up in the morning."

"You," said Frank admiringly, "are one crazy bastard."

What's the rule in covering for a friend?

"Never rat on a rat."

This was Bogart's motto, actually — Bogart, whom Frank worshipped. The words were even emblazoned on the official coat of arms for Bogie's Holmby Hills Rat Pack, the legendary fifties living room drinking society — and precursor to Frank's Las Vegas fraternity. (The elaborate insignia featured a rat gnawing on a human hand; members wore gold rat pins with rubies for eyes.) Bogart's was the first and only Rat Pack that mattered to Sinatra, who was nevertheless elected Pack Leader. But it was Bogie who did the real leading back then. "It was *his* booze," said Frank. (Even then, it was Jack Daniel's for all.) Bogart led by example and Frank followed, studying his wry and subtle swagger, then characteristically enlarged and embellished upon what he saw. Frank's pluck amused Bogie, who once said of his younger friend, "He's a hell of a guy. He tries to live his own life. I like his style."

Getting Bogie, Frank-Style: After making *The Caine Mutiny*, in which the Bogart character Captain Queeg madly fingered an ever-present set of copper ball bearings, the great actor could no longer stand their infernal clattering. For peace, he repaired to his beloved sailboat, the *Santana*, on which Sinatra had hidden hundreds of ball bearings that rattled across the deck with the first broken wave. "I could have killed Frankie at first," said Bogart. "But it was a hell of a gag."

HOW THE RODENTS CAME TO BE: The Bogarts — Betty Bacall and her heroic husband — lived on Mapleton Drive in a swell pocket of Beverly called Holmby Hills. During the

Bogie and Bacall

early fifties, if their porch light blazed late at night, carousers were welcome. Usual suspects included Judy Garland, David Niven, Spencer Tracy, agent Irving "Swifty" Lazar, restaurateur "Prince" Michael Romanoff, writer Harry Kurnitz, Van Heusen, and, of course, Frank — always Frank. Said Bogie: "I don't know what it is about this joint; it seems to be a kind of home for him. It's as though he doesn't have a home of his own. We seem to be parent symbols or something. Or maybe it's just that he likes a place where he can relax completely." For some time, the assemblage was known as the Free Loaders Club, for they all came and drank the Bogarts dry, while arguing politics and crooning around the piano.

That designation changed in June 1955, when Noel Coward crossed the pond to play a nightclub engagement at the Desert Inn in Las Vegas — the province of Sinatra. Frank hatched a plot for the group to descend upon the Strip and rally around the visiting Englishman. "When anything is organized by Sinatra," said Niven, "the arrangements are made with legendary efficiency and generosity." They boarded a bus in front of Bogie's house, were plied with champagne and caviar, then were whisked to the airport, whereupon Frank distributed armbands of many colors to be worn for different occasions. "Yellow armbands, follow me!" he said, marshaling them onto the plane. At the Sands, he commandeered a floor of adjoining suites to which only he held the master key ("so as to be able to rout out any potential shirkers," wrote Pack recording secretary Nathaniel Benchley). "He really enjoyed being head man, arranging for everything in his territory," Bacall remembered. For the next four days, he set a grueling pace of decadent living, making sure armbands corresponded with each new lark (cocktail hours, dinners, show hopping), paying for everything, wearing down every reveler but himself. (Judy Garland passed around pep pills to the especially bedraggled.) Came the dawning of the fifth day, it was Lauren Bacall who gazed upon the hung-over carnage of the crew and uttered seven words that would haunt generations to come: "YOU LOOK LIKE A GODDAMNED RAT PACK!"

Ironically, Sinatra was the only one who did not resemble a besotted rat. He simply glistened, fresh as ever.

The following week, back in Los Angeles, their first formal meeting was called to order, upstairs at Romanoff's, whereupon officers were elected. Frank was voted Leader; Bacall was Den Mother; Garland was Vice-President; Bogie opted for Director of Public Relations; and so on. Jack Entratter, who ran the Sands, sent individual gift-wrapped packages for each — inside of which were live white rats, many of them escaping to frighten diners downstairs. This Rat Pack was all about nonconformity, and to hell with anyone who didn't like it. Said Bacall: "We really *stood* for something. We had principles. You *had* to stay up late and get drunk, and all our members were against the PTA. We had *dignity*. And woe betide anyone who attacked one of our members. We *got* them."

THEY STUCK UP FOR EACH OTHER. Liquor capacity notwithstanding, this was probably the only quality that the original Rats shared with their swinging successors. And, by the way: How he and Dag and Sam and company ever got saddled with that name, Frank never really knew. Once Bogie died, there didn't seem much point. The goddamned newspapermen hung it on them like a nostalgic laurel — and there it stayed. But they were there for each other always. To wit: Frank was so wrecked upon learning of Bogart's death, he could not bring himself to perform that night, at the Copacabana, in New York. So Sam jumped in and covered for him. Once asked by the fine, if cynical, writer Richard Gehman to explain his unflagging devotion to his Leader, Sam replied, "Why — because Frank is a very, very, very great man."

(Gehman wrote: "He looked puzzled, as though wondering what on earth would have made me ask that question.") Dean said in 1967: "Frank's my friend. Some time ago, he called me up and said he had a bad throat. I say: 'I'll be right there.' Got an airplane, did two shows for him. Then I flew right back, very happy. Three days later, he calls me again and says, 'My throat is gone again.' I flew back, did two more shows, very happy."

COVERING ASS, ILLUSTRATED: First, understand that Frank Sinatra did not like to be questioned by authority figures. Second, he did not like to be questioned by anyone else, either. "The thing about him is, he's a cop-hater," Bogie said of him. "If you ask him a question, *any* question, he thinks you're a cop." According to legend, when he was a nattily dressed adolescent in Hoboken, policemen would harass him, rough him up, inferring that he had stolen his clothes, which he had not. It stuck in his craw and he would stay angry about it for the rest of his life. Cops, therefore, never thrilled him. (Incidental or not, whenever alarmed by any musical meanderings on the part of performers or players, Sinatra would snap, *"You've got a beat like a cop!"* He especially

loved saying this to Dean, who especially loved muffing songs just to annoy him.)

And so it was, very late one night in the sixties, that he and Dean were confronted by cops. They had drunk their share, and perhaps the shares of many others, at the Villa Capri in Hollywood, then wobbled out to Dean's red Ferrari. Frank, who wobbled less (as usual), told his friend, "Let me drive." Dean said, "No, no, I'll drive, I'm okay." There was no sense arguing with Dag. And so he drove, very badly, into Beverly Hills, where from behind there came a siren and flashing lights. As Dean pulled to the curb, Frank instructed, "Listen, when the cop comes over, you face the windshield or look at me. Don't look at him or he'll smell your breath. Don't say a thing — just let me do the talking." Dag fuzzily nodded:

"Okay, pally, you do the talking."

Two officers made their approach, whereupon Frank stepped out of the passenger door and started making nice. The cops instantly recognized him, but still wanted to see who was behind the wheel. So one trained his flashlight through the driver's window. Sometimes a flashlight can look like a spotlight, if you are Dean Martin and you are lit to begin with. Bathed in beam, Dean took his cue: *"Evvvvv'rybody,"* he sang, *"loves somebody sometime . . ."* Cover blown, he climbed out of the car. Sinatra shook his head in dismay and rolled his eyes. The cops told Dean to walk along a white line. "No way, pally," said Dag. "Not unless you put a net under it."

At which point, Frank gallantly offered to drive Ferrari and friend home. The cops thought better of it. They delivered both of them to their respective doorsteps in the patrol car.

OMERTA is the law by which Sinatra lived. That is to say, by way of mother tongue, the act of keeping one's mouth sealed in circumstances wherein a compatriot might be hastily judged. That is to say, more bluntly, to say nothing. Never would he fink on a pally. He required the same gesture in return. *"Pray silence,"* he would say always, for he liked the way it sounded and liked more what it meant. Then again, sometimes he would just say it to shut up a noisy room.

Dean naturally reciprocated. On the night of his forty-seventh birthday, Frank took him to the Polo Lounge in the Beverly Hills Hotel to make merry. "We were with six other people, mindin' our business, and we were a little loud," Dean recalled. "When we were goin' out the door, there is a couple of guys, and one of 'em says: 'There goes the two loud Dagos.' Well, Frank got there one split-second ahead of me, and he hit one guy, I hit the other, picked him up and threw him against the wall. The cops came. We said we didn't know who did it and walked out. But we did, yeah."

According to one eyewitness, this is exactly what Dean told the cops: "I just looked around and saw this guy laying there, passed out on the floor, and since that's usually *me,* I didn't pay any attention."

Pray silence.

BEING THERE IN THE DARKNESS, 1964: The story is grim, but he faced the grim, could not turn any other way. Behind him for forty years, Bill Miller played piano, on records and on stages, laying essential foundation, charting the course upon which the baritone made history. Miller was his musical right hand, a background hero, a silent partner. They warmed up together, two men alone, one loosening the reed, the other running the scales, behind closed doors, for always. They drank away a thousand nights together, too. Frank called him Suntan Charley, because no man with blood in his veins was ever so pale. Before embarking upon any vocalizing mission he would say, "Go get Suntan."

"Where's Suntan?" he asked, again and again, on this fateful day.

The rehearsal was set for noon. Suntan, who always came early, did not come at all. Then Frank heard.

Bill Miller and his wife and his daughter had been asleep that morning in their Burbank home when the reservoir behind the property burst. The water — ungodly furies of water — crashed down on the house, ripped it apart, swept everything down the hillside. His daughter, quite miraculously, escaped. He and his wife did not. "I flew out, she flew out, cars came through, I thought I was going to drown," he recalls. In flood rapids, he was washed down the street, clung for two hours to the roof of a car in a storm drain, before rescue arrived. Then he lost consciousness.

His wife, he would later learn, was already gone.

Frank was there, at St. Joseph's, when he woke that night, the first face he saw. Frank assured him that his daughter was all right.

"How about my wife?"

"We don't know. Don't worry about a thing, everything will be taken care of."

The next time he awoke, Frank told him. He had gone to the morgue and identified the body. She had been in the water for a long time. For the next thirty-some years, he would shake his head mournfully and say — although never to Bill Miller — "It's a picture I can't get outta my head."

To Miller, he said this: "Bill, if it's any consolation, there wasn't a mark on her."

"Which," Miller says now, "was maybe a lie, I don't know."

He stayed in the hospital for two weeks (all bills paid), then Frank brought him to his Palm Springs place for another two, easing him back to the life that goes on. Then he found him a nice apartment, got it furnished, made sure father and daughter were comfortable readjusting. "He got me a break on the rent, and paid for the first two and last month's security," says Miller.

"Had the secretaries running around buying dishes and housewares. Had the lawyers getting my papers together. The house was cleaned out. Including a coin collection, which, I don't know, was probably stolen by the police. But he came through like a giant."

They made much music to come.

Can a friend ask
too much of
another friend?

"A friend is never
an imposition."

A friend in need is a pest." Thus spake Joe E. Lewis, providing Frank with another tart nugget to quote eternally, if only on nightclub stages. But never for a moment did he believe such a thing. There was nothing he would not do for someone he loved, much less liked. He knew what it felt like to ask for compassion and receive the air. This was when his voice and his woman, Ava Gardner, had quit him, in the early fifties, and suddenly he was broke and he had no career. He would come to characterize this period with one sentence: "It was all Mondays." His rueful recollections:

"I was in trouble, you know? I was busted, a little short, and, I must say, I lost a great deal of faith in human nature because a lot of friends *disappeared*. Everybody disappeared. I don't say it begrudgingly. Because I found something out about people after that. I understood that some people *don't know how to help*. They want to, but they don't quite know how to do it. They're either shy or they're afraid they'll louse it up and make it worse than it is.

". . . I did lay down for a while and had some large bar bills for about a year. But after that I said, 'Okay, holiday's over, Charley, let's go back to work!' And that's when I began to meet these people who had disappeared in my life. Almost all of them, except for one or two dear, dear so-called friends. And I said, 'How are you? How've you been?' And they were astounded, absolutely stunned, that I even spoke to them. That's when I became aware of the fact that perhaps they didn't know how to handle it, they didn't know how to say to me, 'I haven't got much money, but I can lend you X amount of dollars.' Which I didn't want anyway, because I was picking up little

jobs here and there. But they were insecure themselves and didn't know how to handle helping somebody else."

Such insecurity would never plague him. The lesson resonated further: He would never again ask anything of anyone — unless it was someone whom he employed. (And, of them, all he asked for was excellence, not understanding.) He remembered a moment during that time when he reached out for someone's ear for the very last time: "I was in Florida and I was having some problems. And I called a friend. He was a good friend, although he wasn't ever a close friend. And, apparently, I woke him up. And I said, 'Have you got a couple of minutes. I'd like to talk to you about something. Just listen to me for a few minutes, I wanna get something off my chest.' It had nothing to do with him or anything he knew about. But he was rather short with me. And I said, 'I'm sorry I bothered you.' And I hung up the phone. And I never did that again. Fortunately, I never had to do it again."

But his telephone would ring forever — friends needed help, needed hope, needed him — and HE FIXED EVERYTHING. He was less about empathy than about *solution.* "Once his friend, you're a friend for life," wrote director Vincente Minnelli, who was Judy Garland's second husband. "Of course, he's prone to *tell* friends how he'll help them rather than *ask* how he can help. But I suppose that's the prerogative of any leader of the Clan." Or as Burt Lancaster put it: "If you say to Frank, 'I'm having a problem,' it becomes *his* problem."

His responsiveness to others knew no limit: Hard-luck cases never found a softer touch. Should he have heard that anyone — friend or complete stranger — was in desperate straits, he Took Care of It. When George Raft was hit for eighty-five grand in back taxes, Frank forked over a blank check. ("An example of friendship that doesn't happen very often in this world," Raft said.) Actor Lee J. Cobb, whom Frank barely knew, but whose work he admired, was felled by a heart attack at a time when money was scarce. Sinatra swooped in, overtook Cobb's life, settled all debts, invited him to convalesce in his home, got him on his feet again. Usually, however, Frank's deeds were anonymous ones: Hospital bills were mysteriously paid, nuns found new school buses in their yards, impossible negotiations were suddenly resolved, underdogs got jobs, has-beens got second chances, friends of acquaintances were flown to medical specialists for life-saving surgeries, schools got new gymnasiums, churches got new steeples, children got new dogs, jerks got clobbered.

When his mother, Dolly, visited Pope Paul VI in Rome, the pontiff said, in Italian, "Your son is very close to God." She asked what he meant. "Because he does God's work and he does not talk about it."

Tony Bennett recalls a New York night in the late sixties:

"Judy Garland was in trouble at the end of her life. And, at that time, I was about to open at the Waldorf-Astoria Empire Room. It was my first night and I had butterflies and everything. Then, as I was about to go on, I got this frantic call from Judy Garland at the St. Regis Hotel. She was hysterical — 'Tony, I'm being beaten up in my hotel room. If you don't believe me, here's my son Joey.' He was really upset and said, 'It's true. My mom's being beaten up.' I didn't know what to do. I was about to walk onstage and I was trapped.

"My ex-wife said to call Frank, who was

103

in Florida. I managed to get him on the line and told him, 'Judy Garland's being beaten up at the St. Regis Hotel.' He said, 'I'll call you back in fifteen minutes.' So I hung up. Twelve minutes later, Judy called me again and said, 'I ask for help — and now I have five Jewish lawyers in my room and four hundred police out in the street! What's going on?' Then Sinatra called me back two minutes after that and said, *'Is that all right, kid?'* "

FOR THE LOVE OF SAM: When they found each other, Frank was thirty-two and a star; Sam was twenty-two and a supremely talented nobody. And black. But Frank was color blind, always and ever. Years later, onstage, he and Dean teased their young brother mercilessly: "Keep smiling, Smokey, so the spotlight can find you!" Or, "Why don't you be yourself and eat some ribs!" Or, "Hurry up, Sam, the watermelon's gettin' warm!" But that was their hokum, their way of lampooning color barriers during racially fractious times. They called attention to the idiocy of it all by behaving like idiots, as men will. They were equals in black tie. Sam, for his part, happily leaped into Dean's arms each night, so that Dean could waltz forth and deliver the hay-maker: "I'd like to thank the N-double-A-C-P for this award!" (To which Sam always pro-tested, on cue: "Put me down!") And all three loved to mimic the exaggerated comic drawlings of Amos and Andy.

But none of that bore weight upon the love one felt for another. "Sam was the best friend a man could have," said Frank, whose standards were most rigorous. He saw sweet wonder from the start — the sheerest talent imaginable, and that big beautiful heart — back when Sam danced with his father and uncle, as the Will Mastin Trio. When they shared that billing in 1947 at the Capitol, it was Frank who first asked him — not a question, really — "Why don't you sing?" Whereupon Sam began to sing onstage, sing with lung power untold; ex-cept that he emulated Frank while doing so. Frank, again: "It's okay to sound like me — if you're me. You've got to get yourself your own sound, your own style." Sam took note, sailed forth, his own man, enthralling all. Then he lost an eye in a car wreck. He was sleeping in the backseat, trekking from Vegas to L.A., when the collision occurred. His driver lost his teeth, but Sam got the glass eye, hid it under a pirate patch. "The patch is dramatic as hell," Frank told him, bolstering, never missing a beat. The Leader would not permit him self-pity. For solidarity, all the pallies wore eyepatches in the steam room afterward. Frank took him onto the golf course, made him hit balls, regain equilibrium, sent him optometrist charts with notes, *"Practice, practice."* Told him: "You should have a house," then got him a lease on one in the snooty all-white hills above Hollywood; fuck 'em if they didn't like it. "Don't despair," he lectured always, no matter what. For Kennedy, they stood together at the Democratic National Convention, singing the National Anthem, while the Mississippi bloc booed his blackness, as tears spilled on his cheeks. Frank's hand gripped his shoulder: "Those dirty sons of bitches!" the Leader whispered. "Don't let 'em get you, Charley." When he married the Swedish actress May Britt — an interracial tempest that he postponed, as a Pack courtesy, until JFK was elected — Frank was his best man. ("My man Francis," was how he usually put it.) As a wedding gift,

106

Frank picked out an antique loveseat, then had Dean get it reupholstered. Dag chose zebra skin. Frank asked, "Why the hell did you do that?" Dean: "Well, when they sit on it, they won't clash."

They had two fallouts. The first was a misunderstanding over a gentle blurt. Sam had popped off in a 1959 Chicago radio interview, all the while professing his love for Frank: "Talent is not an excuse for bad manners," he said, almost as an aside. ". . . It does not give you a right to step on people and treat them rotten. This is what he does occasionally." His good eye had witnessed a few dark moments, irrational acts of Sicilian ire, that he could not compre-

hend. Frank, who knew his own faults, did not like to hear them broadcast by little brother. But he could not blame him for long. They mended within months.

The second break came in the seventies, when Sam got into the cocaine. The Leader dropped him hard. "Frank didn't want to be an enabler," says Tracey Davis, Sam's daughter. Three icy years passed until a confrontation: "Sam, I'm so fuckin' disappointed in you, with that shit," Frank said. "Dump it. You're breaking your friends' hearts, Sam."

"I'll give it up, Frank," he said, then did. That was all it took.

Late Fifties,

a Hollywood Favor Recalled:

"Once Sammy Davis called me and he said, 'Hey, Leader, you think I got a shot at playing Sportin' Life when they do the movie *Porgy and Bess*?' I said, 'I don't know. I don't think it should be made to begin with.' And I meant it — the opera had been around a billion years and Irving Lazar, the agent, that little fink, sold it to Samuel Goldwyn under some kind of a guise. Anyway, they made the picture.

"So I went to Mr. Goldwyn — who was superb with some of the things he said. For instance, he could never say Marlon Brando's name properly. He called him Marlo Brandon; he would switch things around like that. And I said to him, 'Will you consider Sammy Davis as Sportin' Life?' And he said, 'Vell, I don't know becuss I don't know vat da hell da story's all about.' I said, 'Sam, it's about a guy who's giving dope to people in Catfish Row.' He said, 'Oh. Why don't you talk to Otto Preminger, the director.' And I did. I said to Preminger,

'You'd make him very happy. He's a pretty good performer.' And they gave him the job.

"When he knew he got the job, he bought a watch for Mr. Goldwyn that had everything on it except the planets and a couple of spaceships going by. One of those huge things. But Sammy's one of the most generous people in the whole world. He gave it to him the day he did an audition for Mr. Goldwyn and Mrs. Goldwyn and seven lawyers and the production head of the studio. I asked if I could sit on a stepladder and watch the performance, which was quite wonderful. He jumped on bales of hay, did the whole number, finished up and did a knee slide right up to Goldwyn's face. And he said, 'Mr. Goldwyn, how was it?' Goldwyn said, 'By the vatch you gafe me, it's forty seconds too long.' True story, absolute true story."

Drinking Again

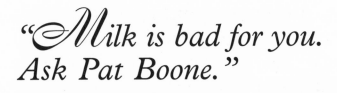

"Milk is bad for you. Ask Pat Boone."

"I may run for the office of President, do it through a write-in ballot. I'll have a slogan on billboards all over the country: **Give me a bottle and a glass and I'll get America off its ass.** *I'll make the Oval room into a big bar that wraps around the walls and put slot machines in the hallways. We'll get off the nut, boy!"*

*Hot damn, boy! I'd like to do a couple of —
I'd like to* GO TO A BAR! *Some saloon somewhere. I want to tell you something: I'm about
up to here in Crown Royal! We snared a batch
of that stuff last night.* Yeecchhh! *It's going
to be* AN AWFUL DRUNK *in Los Angeles for
the next five days. Holy Geez! Suntan Charley
here — my pale pianist Bill Miller — I think,
will appreciate this* WHISKEY. *He would drink
Texaco. It doesn't make any difference to him.
He gets so drunk sometimes that* I CAN
HARDLY SEE HIM. *It's terrible. You've got to
be very careful about the* PEOPLE YOU DRINK
WITH, *you know. We met some strangers last
night; they didn't know how to* HOLD THEIR
BOOZE. *They kept stepping on my fingers all
night long. But* THERE'S NOTHING WRONG
WITH DRINKING. *You know, I have a few
friends who've been picking at me about this
jazz. I mean, if Dean Martin and those guys
can* LUSH IT UP, *I don't see why we shouldn't.*

— MONOLOGUE, JUNE 1957

How stiff should a stiff drink be?

> "Nice and easy. You don't have to beat yourself up. Why be a hero? For what?"

The Leader had a battle cry, which was this: *Fun with everything and I mean* FUN!" For him, drinking meant fun and vice versa. It was not about habit or disease or delirium tremens; it was solely about the act of ring-a-ding-ding, about having the perfect gasser, about living large and lubricated. Then, too, it was about knowing when to knock it off. But, as with every pursuit, his drinking was done always with precision and artful measurement. He perfected the form, then taught those around him, whether they wished this education or not. "That's how I learned to drink," says Don Rickles, "hanging out with him in Vegas and Miami. This was not amateur hour stuff. I still hurt."

When Frank turned forty-two, for instance, Dean crooned to him: "He's the boy who prints all the manuals / On the joy of consuming Daniel's." (This was sung to the Cole Porter tune "You're the Top," re-

worked by treasured Rat Pack lyricist Sammy Cahn as "He's the Wop" — which only Dean could have attempted without sustaining injury.) That private birthday night floated on an amber wave ever undulating, at the Villa Capri in Hollywood. Frank, awash in the merriment, could be heard calling out after more than one number: "Drink your whiskey! I'm trying to get people to drink some whiskey!" That, of course, was what he always tried to do. Years later, he would proudly wear a blue baseball jacket that proclaimed him "Coach of the U.S.A. Drinking Team." He tended to smirk a little when so clad, puffing out his chest just a bit, a peacock with a less-than-secret joke.

"SAY, WHY DON'T WE MIX A LITTLE SAND-WICH?" Dean would say, pushing the portable bar they called the LUNCH CART out onto whatever stage they shared, late in the show. (Variation: "Why don't we mix us a little salad?") At home, Frank could make most any cocktail for anyone and loved

nothing more than doing so. More impressive: "He always remembered what you drank," says Ed McMahon, a frequent Palm Springs house guest and a celebrated inebriant himself. "He'd meet a person once and know that she liked white wine, that he liked martinis, that someone else drank Manhattans. I could never get over that. With all the things in his life he had to remember, that he could remember everybody's drink!" Such was the depth of his commitment to communal carousal.

But what of his own potion? That which, when exceptionally thirsty, he occasionally called the Black Ass of Jack Daniel? Oh, the particulars! This was science, children. His only enemies in the process were zealous bartenders and ice and water, elaboration on which shortly follows.

How he liked it: Always three or four ice cubes, two fingers of Jack Daniel's, the rest water, in a traditional rocks glass.

"This," he would say, "is a gentleman's drink."

"This," he would say, "is nice."

And, foremost, he would say: "I don't like the taste if it's too strong."

His men knew this, told bartenders around the world. Still, bartenders wanted to show off, to overserve, to err on the side of generosity. "Basically," says Tony Oppedisano, "I would teach bartenders, 'Don't try to be his friend by pouring heavy and burying him in booze. He doesn't like it that way.' " To wit: Occasionally, when Frank himself poured incorrectly, he would groan, "*Yeeesh,* that's a *brown* mother I made! Looks like Sammy Davis in a glass."

The glass, by the way, could not be a tall highball glass or a large glass. "He didn't want a bucket," says Tony O. Only a traditional squat old-fashioned, or rocks, glass would do. Whenever he encountered any especially well-designed ones, always with leaded bases, he would order his men to buy him a dozen. A good glass pleased him greatly. Thus, the Sinatra glassware collection became voluminous. When holding his glass, he would usually cup it elegantly from below, with a cocktail napkin, preferably linen. He drank right-handed.

Other lessons:

He would never drink a drink immediately after it was poured.

Tony O: "He'd let it settle a little bit. Let the ice sink in. He said he wanted to let the flavors blend."

Hank Cattaneo: " 'Let it die down,' he'd

117

say. In hotels, I'd instruct them that his Jack Daniel's be brought to him the minute he sits down. For martinis we would wait, of course. But the Daniel's had to come immediately. And there had to be a bowl of ice sitting on the table in front of him. He wants to always keep it fresh, to chill whatever he's drinking."

Of Ice Cubes, Love and Hate: He was a man passionate about ice. Random evidence: He once spoke admiringly of Cole Porter's punctilious snobbery: "I liked it. I'm a snob. I am. Aren't we all, to a certain extent? I mean, I won't tolerate certain things, like being crowded into corners. And *not enough ice in the drink!*" From *Time* magazine, August 1955: "Frankie loves the clink of ice in well-filled glasses." Onstage, mid-seventies, tasting a vodka, recoiling: "Can't this place afford an ice bucket?" The following night, he reported, "I had a hot vodka here last night and like to burn my bird off!"

The other side of the cube: He sat at the bar of the Boston Four Seasons Hotel, considering the ice-laden Daniel's placed before him. He reached into the glass and began plunking cubes onto the bar. The bartender asked: "Is there a problem, Mr. Sinatra?" Quietly, he explained, "No, but with all this ice, I figure we're supposed to go skating here or something. That's not my sport." He left himself four.

He was an ice-tongs fellow, did not like to touch a cube that would touch his lips or anyone else's. A large spoon would also suffice for transference. He was not, however, above pelting a *paisan* with a cube to gain attention or simply to annoy. Ice often amused him. Ritualistically, Jilly would throw a bucket of ice cubes in the air and catch them on descent. He recounted: "Frank says, 'Hey, Jilly, throw the ice cubes!' So I do it. He gets a kick out of it. Anything I can do to take the tension off the guy . . ."

Of Water and Pure Hate: He liked to say that he was as old as water. The way he felt about aging was the same way he felt about water. "I hate water!" he always avowed. "Even my shower's got club soda in it." Water was a prop. In performance and in recording studios, he would call for it, take a sip, then say: "It really is water! I thought you'd be nice to me." Then: "I do hope someone takes a picture of me drinking water." On a *Tonight Show* hosted by Joey Bishop in October 1965, when Dean and Frank were guests, Dean found himself sipping the dread liquid. "I ain't had water since I was seventeen!" he said. "That's real *water!* You ever see what that does to your shoes?" Joey: "You are really a friend, to drink water for a guy!" Frank: "I think he's nuts myself!"

"Frank disdains water," Hank Cattaneo says. "He might rinse his mouth with it after brushing his teeth, but that would be it. If it wasn't mixed with Jack Daniel's, he wasn't too interested."

He never drank a water-back. How the mere notion appalled him! If a waiter placed a glassful before him, he would snap: "What's this! I'm *thirsty,* not *dirty!* Take it away. Now."

WHAT IS THE MOST OFFENSIVE THING THAT CAN HAPPEN TO A MARTINI?

"Warm Vodka.
There's nothing worse."

*W*henever he gave his Daniel's a rest, he turned to vodka, Stolichnaya specifically. He always drank it on the rocks, except in martinis, which were always up and cold and very dry. On the night of his "retirement" performance, June 14, 1971, at the Los Angeles Music Center, he fidgeted in his dressing room, worrying about his reed. "I'd like a vodka," he told somebody. "Either that or a cup of hot tea." Pause. "Better get booze. Forget the tea." Thinking medicinally, he then squeezed an entire half-lemon into it for fortification. Ordinarily, a twist would do.

But his belief in the healing power of potato alcohol was most sincere. When his photographer Ted Allan split his head open in the swimming pool of Mexican President Alemán, Sinatra leaped into action. "Frank ran across the patio, grabbed a bottle of vodka, and poured it all over me," Allan recalled. "This stopped the bleeding immediately. He was that kind of guy." When Elvis Presley was mysteriously hospitalized in Memphis during the seventies, Frank publicly announced, "I'll send him a bottle of booze and he'll get well." (Another remedy of a different color: Gregory Peck once observed him soaking his aching feet in a pan of whiskey. "You have to like a man like that," said Peck.)

VODKA, OF COURSE, HAD ITS OTHER USES. There were always Bloody Marys in his repertoire, a favorite afternoon eye-opener. In the Kennedy White House, he taught the maitre d' how to make them properly, so as to please the young President. At the Sands in Vegas, he would order up three hundred at a time, when he flew in groups of his friends. And vodka always had a place in his martinis, when gin did not appeal to him, which it often did not.

He drank martinis only before dinner, never during or after, and rarely more than two. Martinis were to be taken seriously and made perfectly dry. Once, in 1949, he slugged a belligerent bartender who told him, "If you want it so special, mix it yourself." He usually did. *"It's 'tini time!"* he would bellow late afternoons on the Indiana set of *Some Came Running*, whereupon Dean and Shirley MacLaine came running, to his trailer, where the olive soup awaited. During the making of *From Here to Eternity*, he turned his hotel room into a martini lounge for Montgomery Clift, Deborah Kerr, and Burt Lancaster. The nightly ritual, as recalled by Lancaster: "He had a refrigerator in his room and he would open it and there would be these iced glasses. And now he would prepare the martinis. He'd put on a waiter's white apron, and serve the martini with some snacks while we were getting ready to go to an eight o'clock dinner. When you finished your martini, he would take the glass away from you and open the icebox and get a fresh cold glass."

His perfect martini: Stoli or excellent British gin, well-stirred or shaken in ice, with the tiniest drop of vermouth, served in cold glass and crowned by two olives. The olive was the fruit of symbolic resonance for him. Back when bobby-soxers swooned and he was bone-thin, Bing Crosby told him, "Sinatra, you, sir, are so completely emaciated that you could stroll through an olive without even disturbing the pimento." As wiry little Private Angelo

Maggio, in *From Here to Eternity*, for which his Oscar and professional resurrection followed, he rolled olives. Like dice, he rolled them. Two of them, across a bar. Spirits high, he called out, "Hey, Seven!" They landed the only way they could have, two pimentos beaming: "Aw, SNAKE EYES!" he groaned. "That's the story of my life!" Later he privately reprised the act for friends.

Of teetotaler Joey Bishop, he would tease, "Do you know that he has the distinction of being the only man alive who has ever eaten a dry olive?" Bishop looked baffled. Then Frank would explain, pointing over toward Dean, as contrast: "That means, Charley, that *he* drinks martinis with *wet* olives in 'em all the time." (Frank never really understood teetotalers.)

He always shared an olive from his martini. This was something of a sacred act, performed not casually but with an air of Eucharist. The young actor Chazz Palminteri was invited to a dinner party at the Sinatra Malibu beach house. He stood with other guests out on the patio. "Suddenly, everybody else walked inside to get something to eat," Palminteri would recall. "And I was alone with Frank, looking out at the water. He asked me to get him a martini, and then he asked me to share his olive. I didn't know what he meant. He said, 'Come on, Chazz, share my olive,' and he held up the martini. He took out the toothpick with two olives on it, and he gave it to me. So I took one of the olives and he took the other, and we both threw them in our mouths, and he tapped me on the back and said, 'Let's go inside.' I found out later that that's a sign of friendship. I will never forget taking an olive from Frank Sinatra."

Snake eyes, split. Story of his life.

There Was One Exception, Martini-Wise: In a 1962 recording, titled, most appropriately, "Nothing But the Best (Is Good Enough for Me)," by Johnny Rotella, Frank sings, "I like a new Lincoln with all of its class; / I like a martini and burn on the glass." *Burn on the glass!* This was a barely veiled tribute to the legendary martini at Chasen's restaurant in Beverly Hills, as created by the great bartender Pepe Ruiz. It was called, if a bit unfortunately, the FLAME OF LOVE MARTINI — or simply, and better, Pepe's Flame — of which Frank happily consumed hundreds over the years.

Pepe's recipe: "You swirl a few drops of La Iña sherry in a chilled stem glass and pour it out. Then squeeze a strip of orange peel into the glass and flambé it with match. Throw away the peel. Now fill the glass with ice to chill again, then throw that out. Add the vodka, then flambé another orange peel around the rim. Now throw out the second burnt peel. Then just stir it gently. And drink, drink."

Dean Martin, poetically enough, was responsible for the Flame, according to Pepe. Dean sat at the end of the bar three or four nights a week — this was during the sixties — sipping martinis that bored him. "I'm so sick and tired of the same thing!" Pepe says Dean said. Pepe spent three weeks experimenting, until he hit pay dirt. Dean came in and Pepe stood before him igniting orange rinds. "I really surprise the guy," says Pepe. Dean sipped and declared, "This is the greatest thing I ever put in my mouth!" (Give or take, one could only guess.)

Frank came in and found equal bliss. "Holy Christ!" he said, gleeful at the discovery. When he held an anniversary party at Chasen's years later, he had Pepe prepare sixty-five Flames for his guests, thus requiring much inferno on the premises. Pepe recalls, "I said, 'Frank, why you do this to me?' He said, 'I want to see if you can do it without burning down this joint.' But that was Frank. Beautiful guy."

SHOULD A MAN
FEEL COMFORTABLE
DRINKING WHITE
WINE?

> "I don't drink that sissy stuff,
> for Christ's sake! *You* drink
> white wine!"

A man has to eat. And when he eats,
then he will drink the wine. He once sang,
on record in 1971, "I Will Drink the Wine,"
a strident anthem whose opening lyric gave
him little other option: "Someone said drink
the water; but I will drink the wine." And
so he would drink the wine, aged cases of
it in his Palm Springs cellar or in a locker
at the Wine Merchant in Beverly Hills, and
it was very good, very expensive wine. A
thousand dollars per bottle tended to be his
median. "I've learned to appreciate the finer
things in life," he would say, not apologetically. "I work hard. I deserve them." So he
drank them. Only with friends.

RED, he loved. French and Italian. Preferably PETRUS and MOUTON ROTHSCHILD
and GAJA and, in a pinch, MARGAUX. At
home, on his seventy-ninth birthday, he
poured out a couple bottles of '57 Rothschild

127

without blinking. WHITE he would grudgingly tolerate in deference to fish and poultry and the judgment of others. But only MONTRACHET or CARTE CHARLEMAIGNE were deemed suitable to his particular palate.

Often, while in such Dionysian revelries, he spoke of the wine he was given as a school kid in Hoboken, bad Bogadalino wine: "When I was a boy, we used to get hot wine just to keep us warm on the winter mornings. Our parents thought it would help us survive the six or seven blocks we walked to school. And everybody showed up in the classroom bombed! Eight years old, I swear to God! Kids would walk into class with the red cheeks, staggering, 'Guh-marrning-teasherrr, howwaarryooo t'day' . . . And then on Sunday mornings, during the Masses, we would sneak a little bit more from the Communion jugs — and get a smack in the face. There was a guy at St. Ann's church, he had the funniest accent I ever heard in my life — he used to say, *'You drink again-a, eh? You gonna be a bum!'* But the wine was too sweet. Even then, I wanted Chateau Lafitte."

CHAMPAGNE, meanwhile, was only for the indulgence of women. Upon toasting, he would take one sip, for luck, then put it down and leave it there. (Carbonation was not his friend — he even preferred his Coca-Cola flat.) Otherwise, if pressed to drink further, he always added ice cubes, which, like the martini olives, he would ceremoniously share. One of his former dinner partners recalled such an instance: "Using his spoon, he lifted some ice cubes from his tulip-shaped glass and transferred them to mine. I couldn't help being overwhelmed by one sudden, giddy thought: My God, I'm drinking Frank Sinatra's ice cubes!"

He had this effect on people.

What is a good hell-raising toast?

"Here's to the confusion of our enemies!"

$\mathcal{I}$t does not matter what one toasts, as long as one toasts. His first taste on any night would always be preceded by the clinking of glasses. More often than not he would employ the Italian words *Cent'anni*, which, according to Tony Oppedisano, "means we should live a hundred years. Later he rethought it, figuring he was getting a little close to that number: 'Hey, I'm not getting any younger here.' So he made it *Cento e due*. He said, 'Then when I get *there*, I'll renegotiate.' "

A Sinatra toast is always one of invincibility. "It's post time, ladies and gentlemen," he would say, invoking the phrase of his friend, the drinking man's comedian Joe E. Lewis, whom he portrayed in *The Joker Is Wild*. Whereupon he would drink to the crowd at hand, large or intimate. Long ago, he began toasting concert audiences thusly: "May you all live to be four hundred years old and may the last voice you hear be mine." As decades passed, he would increase the proposed collective longevity — four hundred years became seven hundred fifty became one thousand became *five* thousand. When he was feeling especially contented, his toasts were simply largesse maximus: "I wish you an abundance of health and goodness and sweet things and sweet dreams, no nightmares, and I wish you lemonade in the shade in July and all that other jazz, and huggin' and kissin' and peace forever in your time and for your children and their children and *their* children and God bless us all! Cheers! *Salud! Cent'anni!* There — that'll hold you till Sunday. . . . "

His New Year's Resolution Toasts

Composed to confront 1980 as only he could — read onstage at Caesar's Palace in Las Vegas. A timeless sampling:

- Give up drinking all day on February 30.

- Not get upset with the crummy press unless they deserve it and I will be the judge.

- Pay my income taxes with rubber checks so I can bounce them around April 15 the way the IRS bounces us around the rest of the year.

- Help little old ladies and Dean Martin cross the street whenever I can.

- Stop referring to the colored cat who sings "Candy Man" as Smokey, treat him with the dignity he deserves, and refer to him by his given name, Sambo Davis Jr.

- Be kind to dumb animals including all cats, dogs, and reporters from the *National Enquirer*.

- Stop losing in the casino, unless they stop keeping a closer eye on me.

- Play more golf and give up using golf carts to conserve power. That way it will give more exercise to my throne-bearers.

- Do everything I can to help the best man get elected President even if it means digging up Millard Fillmore, Abe Lincoln, or one of those other cats — or Tom Mix.

- Do more to help my country and start by sending the President and Congress tubes of Krazy Glue to brush their teeth with.

- Stop smoking — as in the shower.

HOW DOES THE SMOKER PREVAIL IN A WORLD OF NONSMOKERS?

> "Tell 'em, You die your way, I'll die mine."

*W*hen vices intermingle: "The only guy who can hurt you is yourself," he would lecture himself and others alike. On one bitch of a night in the sixties, he sat forlorn in a Burbank TV studio, the voice but a croak, lamenting that which had gone down the night before: "Drink, drink, drink. Smoke, smoke, smoke. Schmuck, schmuck, schmuck." He would eventually confess, "Smoking is stupid." But he never really stopped, maybe for a few days here and there, most always before recording sessions or big concerts. He was vigilant that way — it was bad for business. If he hit a clam while making a record, he'd grumble, "That was an *old* Chesterfield that just came up on me — around 1947, it felt like."

Booze and smoke, of course, were sentries of his nocturnes. Quite naturally, there would always be smoke encircling him during saloon song performances. That was theatrical. (Lighting up, onstage, 1961: "If you're all gonna blow smoke at me, I'm gonna blow some back at you. Smoke, Frank. Go ahead, it's good for your throat. Go ahead, smoke some more.") And always there were cigarettes on the fingers of the pallies when they gagged it up together at the Sands. "I was gonna light this," he'd say to Dean and Sam, "but standing next to you two, I don't need to." He did not like to smoke in movies, however, and this was for practical reasons. It was too hard to match the length of a burning cigarette, while shooting take after take. He tried to convince Sam of this during the making of *Ocean's Eleven.* "You can't take one of these from shot to shot unless you're Bob Mitchum," he scolded. Frank called Sam Smokey the Bear, with both affection and disdain — he smoked too goddamned much.

Dean was equally dedicated to the habit. "I quit every night," he liked to say. Often, he would watch Frank smoke onstage and ask him incredulously, "Don't you inhale *at all?*"

In fact, he did not.

Frank never inhaled, saving his reed while maintaining *la figura,* the appearance, cupping them like Bogie did. After Lucky

Strikes and Chesterfields, he took up Camels, always unfiltered. Rarely did he take more than four drags before extinguishing. And even more rarely would he smoke before nightfall. "I smoke usually after dinner — or during cocktail period," he said. "Yeah! That's the time — cocktail period!" Always he handled cigarettes with style. He liked to keep them loose from the pack in his right coat pocket, extracting each with effortless sleight of hand. The little gold Dunhill lighter was inside the right change pocket. Ever quick to light any woman's cigarette, he opened the flame silently beneath the tip. The movement was fluid, almost unnoticeable, a lost art.

Cigars didn't interest him terribly. Nor did they offend. "Fresh air makes me throw up," he once attested. "I can't handle it. I'd rather be around three Denobili cigars blowin' in my face all night." Before marrying Barbara Marx, he would occasionally partake during poker games with the boys. He favored big Cuban Lonsdales, could even be seen chomping them in *Four for Texas* with Dean. Equally incongruous: He actually liked to smoke a pipe. Bing would give them to him, a bestowal of no small symbolism and regard. He puffed them in contemplative moments, while painting at his easel or attending a Dodger game. "It helps me think straight," he said.

And Then There Was Marijuana: He called it tea, as in *Let us smoke us a little tea,* and he hated it. On band buses in the forties, thick tea clouds enveloped and stupefied him. "The cigarette smokers and the guys who smoked a little grass always sat in the back of the bus, where the windows were open," he would recall. "But they didn't realize that the slipstream was blowing it back into the bus again. You could see the guys down in front, who were partially square, take a deep breath once in a while when the smoke would come blowing through. It was absolutely hysterical." Tommy Dorsey's great piano man Joe Bushkin finally tempted Frank to try some: "He was the first cat to lay a roach on me, when I was about nineteen years old," he said. "That's when I went to whiskey immediately after that."

Mia Farrow, his young third wife, smoked pot, about which he was not crazy. But this was the middle sixties, years of mad reefer and happenings most groovy. One night they went to The Factory, an L.A. discotheque that Sammy owned in part; Mia wandered off and he stood at the bar with his guys. At which point, a fellow with lit pupils approached and inquired, "Hey, Frankie . . . you got any *grass* on ya?" Frank stiffened: "Yeah, pal, I got plenty of grass. It's at home — on my *lawn*." Whereupon the men of Sinatra hoisted the fellow by his elbows and deposited him elsewhere.

WHAT IS THE MOST DEPENDABLE CURE FOR A HANGOVER?

"Don't drink to begin with."

"Dean and I did a lot of jokes about drinking. But let's face it: If we had actually drunk as much as people said we did, do you think we could have made movies all day and done shows at night — which we did? I would not recommend that anyone else live life that way. You have to know what you can handle."

*H*angovers feared him. His metabolism knew no such thing. "He doesn't get hangovers — he *gives* them," says television producer George Schlatter. "He's a carrier." If ever he felt lousy, he rarely said so; usually he would place blame elsewhere. Early one morning at the Waldorf, for instance, he called Robert Wagner, with whom he had closed "21" the night before. Frank asked him, "What the hell was the name of that last place we went to? I think they *poisoned* me!" Sam saw him suffer — and that was just once! — after the night Frank wanted to punch out John Wayne. The Duke had briefly come over to Frank's table at a party and hovered uncomfortably close. "You're *leaning* on me!" Frank complained. (He detested being crowded.) Duke grinned and beat it and, an hour later, Frank — who'd uncharacteristically gotten himself "about ten sheets to the wind" (Sam's words) — decided to settle the score. He confronted the big guy, who just lifted the Leader and set him aside. Sam went to the house the next day, he recalled, and "out of the back came Frank, staggering to the bar. He said, *'I gotta get a Ramos gin fizz!'* "

The Ramos gin fizz was the only solution. The hissing hair-of-dog! A legendary New Orleans shaken mix of lemon juice, egg white, powdered sugar, orange flower water, cream, and gin, topped with soda — it lined the stomach thickly and sent pixilated juniper straight to the head. Frank ordered them by the tray, by the dozen, plied his pallies with them inside the Sands steam room, whose humble walls absorbed the toxins of the

FS pretends for photographer Phil Stern

gods. (Strangely, Dean's cure was malted milk.) For hangovers, and all bodily setbacks, Frank prescribed combat: "You had to fight your way through them." He believed in rallying, would actually raise an Alka-Seltzer flag above the Palm Springs compound on certain tough mornings-after. (On many nights previous, he flew a Jack Daniel's flag, the portent of pain to come.)

"You're not drunk if you can lay on the floor without holding on," he'd often say, quoting Joe E. Lewis, who knew that horizontal hold all too well. Whenever serious inebriation overtook Sinatra, it did not readily show. Never was he a sloppy drunk, nor was he one to stumble or slur words. Quite the opposite: "With Frank, it only made him a little more punctilious," recalled artist friend Paul Clemens. "His posture was very erect, his speech was *more* articulate, and his manners were more courtly." His clothes remained crisp, his gait remained purposeful. The darkest manifestation of drink, alas, was his temper, which could, on the odd occasion, reach flashpoint in a microsecond. "It was Jekyll-and-Hyde time," Swifty Lazar would write. "Jimmy Van Heusen once gave me some good advice on how to handle Frank if he's drunk: Disappear!"

Aware of these eruptions, aware of all, he was not always remorseful, for that would suggest weakness. But he understood. He knew. There was the night at the Sands, for instance, that Sammy got himself loaded, vituperatively so, and he tore into his Leader with hot invective, mindless cussing. Frank silently withstood it. Sam stormed off and awoke the next day to learn of what he had done, which was something he had never done before. If anything, he was always a tad too worshipful. So he marched to Frank's suite and faced the music: "Good morning," said Sam, "I understand I made a fool of myself last night. I would like —" Frank stopped him, told him to sip some coffee, then said, "Look, we've all done exactly what you did last night, but if you can't handle it, don't do it. Now, what are we going to do today?"

He knew.

He knew tricks, too. When he drank at parties, when he appeared to be consuming tens of beverages, glass after glass after glass, he was not. He once told his daughter Nancy this secret: "You take a couple of sips and you put it down in one corner and you walk away and they give you another drink and they think you're drinking a lot. It's important. They think you're as relaxed as they are, but you don't have to drink."

Tony Oppedisano, who witnessed this phenomenon repeatedly, says, "He'd have drinks all over the place. People saw him order fourteen drinks, but if you added 'em up, he drank maybe two altogether."

Which was not to say that he employed this trick every night. For he also knew when he had had enough, which he often did. But he would not confess it. Instead, he projected his saturation point onto others. He would gaze at whoever was left in his midst at whatever hour of dawn. And he would tell them: "I think you better put it in the bag." Meaning: *You are drunk. Go to bed.* Occasionally, a miraculously lucid companion would protest otherwise, until Frank's head began nodding in flirtation with slumber. And then it was clear whose bag truly beckoned.

Style

When you wear those duds,
Duds with white tie and studs,
Watch those dolls linin' up, single-file!

— FROM THE SONG "STYLE,"
SUNG BY FS, DEAN MARTIN,
AND BING CROSBY IN
ROBIN AND THE SEVEN HOODS, 1964,
LYRICS BY SAMMY CAHN

Got my tweeds pressed,
Got my best vest,
All I need now is the girl.

— FROM THE SONG
"ALL I NEED IS THE GIRL," 1959,
LYRICS BY STEPHEN SONDHEIM
AND JULE STYNE

FRANK (Fingering Sam's wardrobe): *What is this — with the tie down and the collar open? Where did you learn that? At the Flamingo? That went out with button shoes! And, beside that, what are you doing in a cockamamie street suit? You're supposed to wear a dinner jacket! Now go on up to your room and put on your little ol' tuxedo, Sam!*

SAM: *Hold it! What're you,* Esquire *magazine? As far as my attire is concerned, Frank — let's get one thing straight now: I'm thirty-seven years old! I will change my clothes when I get good and ready!*

FRANK: *Are you ready?*

SAM: *Yes, Frank.*

FRANK: *Well, then, go upstairs and change your clothes.*

(Sam returns twenty minutes later, properly attired.)

FRANK: *Ahh, now you look like a little pussycat in your nice dinner jacket, see? With your tie all buttoned up nicely!*

DEAN: *Hey, how come we wear pants and he wears leotards?*

— A RAT PACK FASHION MOMENT, ONSTAGE AT THE SANDS, 1962

**How do you know
when a hat looks
right on you?**

"When no one laughs. My favorite was the one I wore in *Pal Joey*. I was so crazy about that suit from the movie, I didn't want to wear the coat over it — and that's why I put it over my shoulder."

*W*hither the hat? "No one wore a hat like Dad did," says Tina Sinatra. Indeed, rarely has any head covering had as much impact as his. The hat was his crown, cocked askew, as defiant as he was. To be like him required a hat — and, correspondingly, hat sales jumped across America and beyond. Frank had snap-brims for all seasons, made exclusively and expensively by Cavanaugh — pristine felts of black and gray for cool sojourns; porous palmettos and straws with wide bands of pastel for balmy climes. They went where he went, accentuating the bounce of his step. Late at night, around piano bars, for amusement, he would squash them onto the heads of drunken pals and make the coronated sing his songs to

him. He knew what the hats stood for. Now no one in the family seems to know where they have gone. Said Eydie Gorme, in 1995: "He recently told me he missed wearing those hats so much. He loved being able to take it off, give it to a hatcheck person, put it back on, tip it, push it down, push it up."

HE WORE THEM FROM BOYHOOD, the scrawny Hoboken dandy, swaggering along rough pavement, ever ready to deck anyone who knocked one off his head. Hats later rode band buses with him, pulled over his face, so as to promote snoozing across interstates. But it was during the fifties — the Capitol years — that his hats became iconic and indelible. Quite famously, he liked to make records in them. From *Time* magazine, 1955: "As Sinatra stands up to the mike, tie loose and blue palmetto hat stuck on awry, his cigarette hung slackly from his lips, a mood curls out into the room like smoke." (That year, he owned twenty hats in all.) He appeared behatted on twenty Capitol album covers alone, then on another thirteen covers for his own Reprise record label in the sixties. He played constantly with angles and tilts, offhandedly practicing a geometry of attitudes. The higher he pushed it back, the more vulnerable he became. The lower he pulled it, the more debonair and intimidating. Entering the studio to record the *Softly, As I Leave You* album in 1964, he was thusly captured by the majestic liner note writer Stan Cornyn: "He looks smart, what your mother used to call 'natty.' His wide-banded hat is tipped back, one inch off straight flat." That was the all-business angle.

The Favored Slant: His back brim always curled aloft and the front snap was tugged down a couple of inches above his right brow. The move required two hands — aft hiking up, fore pulling down.

Such nuances were studied by young men everywhere, hoping to achieve through effort that which Sinatra achieved through none. Like a torpedo nose, the tip of his hat navigated his movements, always brisk, issuing an air of purpose. Not that he thought about this for a moment: "He just put it on," says Nancy Jr., simply. (As a girl, she would snatch his hats off his head and wear them herself, parading around the house or studio.) "It was like an extension of him," she goes on. "The funny thing is, he wore them as a response to his receding hairline; it was just an easier way of dealing with it in public. He didn't realize what a tumult he would start."

It was only when his hair had grayed, in the seventies, that the hats disappeared. Privately, he took to golf caps and baseball caps. But if he wasn't wearing casual clothes, he wasn't wearing any hats at all. It was an acknowledgment, unconscious and barely noticed, that the world had changed, that jauntiness belonged to another time. No one else was wearing hats, either. And so he began missing them more than ever.

HOW DO YOU KNOW WHEN YOU'VE PICKED THE RIGHT BARBER?

> "When you leave the shop and no one hands you a hat, you're okay."

Every man has an Achilles' heel. Frank Sinatra's would reside beneath his Cavanaugh. By the time he reached his late twenties, his hairline had begun its certain retreat; his forehead, like his star, was in full ascent. He accepted it with humility at first: "I'll never sing like Bing, I know I don't compare. / I'll grant them that he's got voice, if they'll grant me that I've got hair." He crooned this to servicemen in 1944, getting big and knowing laughs. Later, it rankled him, as it would any man of virility. Dean, whose locks were thick, tried to bolster his pally, somewhat, in public: "Frank's so strong. He's a little bald, but that's all." Marlon Brando, who tested Frank's patience with his ponderous Method acting in *Guys and Dolls*, once teased: "He's the kind of guy that when he dies, he's going up to heaven and give God a bad time for making him bald."

For business reasons — bald troubadours flutter few hearts — he fought back, although he knew that everyone else knew what he was doing. The toupees were an open secret. He disliked wearing them, didn't care if friends saw him without. "I once took a close shot of him without his toupee, and he never complained," recalled Ted Allan, the renowned photographer whom he employed. "It gets to be a bore wearing wigs. With Frank, it was just professional." Far more important was that the decoys were as carefully maintained as the waning tuft God gave him, always neatly trimmed and short, very short. Unkempt hair on any man annoyed him — especially on his men. Of an overgrown Sam, onstage, 1962: "Wait'll he digs me with a pair of shears! Oh, boy, you're gonna get yours in the morning!" Whenever he spotted a stray hair in revolt on his own head, he went on attack, wielding scissors like a scythe. "He'd start to snip and snip," says Hank Cattaneo, who regularly witnessed such fussing on the road. "Sometimes he'd get so carried away that he'd oversnip and get too close to the scalp."

"Cleanliness was paramount to Dean and Frank," wrote Shirley MacLaine, distaff mascot to the fellas. "I'd sit in their suite,

fascinated at the spectacle of them primping for a night out. They didn't mind my watching them. They thought of me as a loyal pet." Frank loved that Dean, like him, was immaculate and beautifully turned out. Both had rituals of grooming, timed to the second without variation. Once dressed, both pawed their presentation repeatedly — adjusting jacket, flattening tie, shooting cuffs, picking lint, chamoising shoes. Nancy says of her father: "He was rarely pressed for time. He always allowed himself enough time to do what he had to do in order to get out of the house." Dean was a lifelong electric shaver; Frank was a straight-blade man, later graduating to safety razors, then to disposables, finally to electric. In the early fifties, he tried mustaches, which grew pencil-thin and miserably wispy. Jackie Gleason once bounded out onto Frank's television show with a floor brush in hand: "I'm gonna scrub off that *dirty upper lip* you've been sporting for the last eight weeks!" Frank: "That's not a dirty upper lip! That's my mustache! Better to scoop up the cheese in the pizza." Gleason: "I got more hair than that on my cuff!" The mustache was gone the next week.

Sinatra hygiene became the stuff of legends. Showering was something of an obsession, and he'd take no fewer than two a day, usually more. "I accused him of taking so many showers that he scrubbed his hair off," said Ted Allan. Ava Gardner vouched: "Frank was the cleanest man I ever knew, forever changing his clothes and underwear, always showering and washing. If I'd caught him washing the soap it wouldn't have surprised me." As a boy, he carried the scent of soap like a badge of honor, for he washed fastidiously after regular dust-ups with street punks. With maturity, he smelled mostly of witch hazel and YARDLEY'S ENGLISH LAVENDER, always light and fresh. (The Spanish cologne Agua Lavender Puig later became his stalwart.) Dean wore FABERGE WOODHUE. Sam, flamboyant as ever, liked to luxuriate in a bath of LACTOPINE, HERMES, and AU SAUVAGE, then splash on ARAMIS afterward. "Strong colognes drive me out of the room," Sinatra once said, which further evinces his love for Sam. (Frank reportedly had an acute aversion to Aramis — paling only in comparison to his violent hatred of the smell of roasting lamb.) Whenever he disapproved of any pally's fragrance, he would simply state: "What's that shit you're wearing?" He was not one for making subtle points.

Possessed of a manicurist's vigilance, he habitually deployed clippers and emery boards to smooth away the fray of cuticles. After all, he rationalized, he worked with his hands — indeed, with his whole body — punctuating the lyrics he sang with gestures great and small. Some of them, as catalogued in 1990 in *The New Yorker*: "Upper arm pinched against his body, bent elbow, drooping hand. The rhythmic wince. Twirling, dismissive left hand. Pained, sudden, loud stamp, on the beat. Biting the air." Some stage movements had a secret agenda: Using his forefinger, before pointing skyward on musical epiphany, he would graze his brow to eliminate a new bead of sweat. Few people ever saw this, which was the point. Frank Sinatra is not supposed to perspire. Also, when hanging his fist below the waist, he would often stare down at the tip of his thumb. A close friend once asked him why. "You saw me look at my thumb?" said Frank — caught. "I always look at my thumb! Gives me a second to focus." Privately, whenever deep in thought, he stroked his lower lip with a thumbnail.

He believed that a man should never hide his scars. His were carved into the left side of his neck at birth. As legend suggests, he was born all but dead. (For the autobiography he never got around to writing, he decided that one chapter would be called "The Day I Was Born I Nearly Died.") Trapped in his mother's womb, he was clumsily extricated by forceps that tore his face and gave him the marks that would forever remind him of how he fought his way into this life. (Which, he vowed, would be the only way he'd ever leave it.) The scars were who he was. Wrote Nancy Sinatra in her book *Frank Sinatra: An American Legend*: "The struggle of the infant would shape the character and conduct of the boy and remain a motivating force in the man. Perhaps in those few moments lie some of the forces behind the impatience, the steamroller ambition, his exhausting pace, his extravagant style."

Every day that he shaved, he confronted this mortal triumph and reason for being — right there, on the mug in the mirror. "People have suggested to me I ought to hide those scars, but no," he would say. "They're there, and that's that. Why bother?"

WHAT COLOR SHOULD NO REAL MAN WEAR?

"What's the difference?
A color is a color."

Rules for color depended only on the time of day. About those rules, he was adamant. But he knew that no color made a man less manly. "To him, colors enhance life," says Tina Sinatra. He wore pink. He wore lavender. He wore lilac. Orange, he adored. "Orange is the happiest color," he said whenever he saw it. His homes and offices and airplane interiors were awash in it. Orange birds of paradise filled flower vases everywhere around him. He loved to wear orange sweaters, orange bathing trunks, orange sport shirts, and orange oxford-cloth shirts. He would, however, only tolerate orange flecks in his neckties, not much more, for ties were the hallowed province of taste and conservatism. He was crazy about his ties — only silk would do, in muted patterns or dignified stripes; he favored the feel and designs of Sulka, which he learned from George Raft, who wore Sulka everything. Turnbull & Asser impressed him as well. (Later, he launched his own line of neckwear based on his paintings, careful geometric abstracts mostly, nothing loud.) "I've never known a woman who could select neckties I really like," he once said. "I think any gal who could do that, who could pick out a dozen ties I would really like, would pass the supreme test." (Ironically, the only exception was his first wife.)

He never wore brown at night. His rigidity here was notorious. Brown offended him greatly after dark. When he spotted a hapless square whom he chose not to label a Harvey, he would designate him a Charley Brown-Shoes. (There was no excuse for brown shoes past sundown, ever.) He sartorially sized up all men in his midst, scorned them for their sins: Pianist Bill Miller, a.k.a. Suntan Charley, turned up for a gig in the fifties clad brownly. Frank's eyes narrowed at the atrocity: "Brown suit? Brown shoes?" he said, recoiling in horror. Miller: "What's wrong with dark brown?" Frank, issuing the final word: "It's nighttime. You wear dark gray or you wear black. Besides, brown doesn't match your eyes." To emphasize his convictions, he was not above inserting lit firecrackers into the brown shoes of any comrade. Badly scuffed shoes and cockamamie white shoes were equally unsafe. (He made sure new and better replacements were forthcoming.)

Even gray was iffy. Only the deepest of charcoals were barely permissible; lighter shades were not. Dean felt the same way — he shared most all Sinatra predilections of dress. He and Frank wandered onto the set of *The Tonight Show* in October 1965, wearing black, only to find guest host Joey Bishop, Ed McMahon, and most of the band in pale grays. "We wanna ask you fellas — what are you doin' with the gray clothes on?" said Frank. "This is a midnight show! You only go out in daytime with these gray suits." Dean went further: "You guys should be in the balcony. You're supposed to get all dressed for *The Tonight*

Show — and you come out in gray! *Yecchhh!*" Blue was wrong for after-hours, too, unless it was midnight blue. A man, they believed, should blend in with the black sky.

COURT HABERDASHER TO THE RAT PACK was one Sy Devore of Beverly Hills, who trafficked in all that sheened — rayons and mohairs and sharkskins aglimmer. Described in Pack lore as Custodian of the Royal Robes, he ran with the boys and measured their inseams. More importantly, he cut their suits like black knives. The creases held eternally. Bob Hope called Devore "the Don Loper of the mozzarella set." Dean found him first, with Jerry Lewis, and Frank this time took Dag's lead. Elvis Presley did, too. (Elvis worshipped Dean for his sublime cool, would ride his motorcycle past the Martin house on Mountain Drive late at night, awed that his hero slept within.) Devore's threads permitted the pallies to flash much cuff, which was key. Frank took to wearing three-button cuffs when not wearing links. Dean called his cuff links "curbfeelers."

Both men would have rather died than have their clothes mussed. Loved ones exempted, Frank could not bear to be touched unless he touched first. After he sang the National Anthem at the 1956 Democratic National Convention (Adlai Stevenson was his candidate), an elderly man grabbed his arm and genially asked, "Aren't you going to sing 'The Yellow Rose of Texas' for us, Frank?" Sinatra reportedly gave him frost and said, "Take your hand off the suit, creep." He was unwittingly addressing Speaker of the House Sam Rayburn. Such tales of trespasses gave weight to the words of his former boss, Tommy Dorsey: "Frank is the most fascinating man in the world, but don't stick your hand in the cage."

His pride of ownership, garment-wise, started in Hoboken. Of course. There, a Neapolitan Fauntleroy, he was known, a bit derisively, as Slacksey O'Brien — no boy's pants were ever fancier. By the time he entered high school, he had thirteen sport coats. "My mother bought me my first suit when I was fourteen or fifteen," he would say. "Later, I got a job as a copy boy at the *Jersey Observer* and I used the money to buy clothes. The clothes we wore back then were described as spiffy, nifty, and swell." By the dawn of the sixties, he had over one hundred fifty suits, and he would describe them only as *sharp*. A few years later, he embraced his Chairmanship fully and abandoned Sy Devore for the British banker styles of Carroll & Co., also of Beverly Hills, as well as Dunhill and other Savile Row imports. Old Joe Kennedy, Jack's father, could not fathom the extent of the Sinatra wardrobe. "FRANCIS, HOW MANY SUITS DO YOU NEED?" he once asked him at Hyannisport. The question fell on deaf ears. Frank's only response: "Why do you call me Francis?"

"I AM A SYMMETRICAL MAN, ALMOST TO A FAULT," he confessed one day. "I demand everything in its place. My clothing must hang just so." Wiseacres of his acquaintance likened the expanse of his closet to that of the Polo Grounds. They were mistaken. "His closets were always rather small, even by today's standards," says Nancy. "He was always going through them and organizing and cleaning out and weeding out and giving away. He never had too many of any one thing, just the right amount." (After all, at one point, he could divide his suits into the closets of five homes: Palm Springs, Beverly Hills, New York, London, and Acapulco.) His organizational skills were exemplary: "It's called 'anal retentive,' " says Tina Sinatra. "I remember the closets most. I would marvel at the way things were hung together in categories. Sweaters were folded on shelves; the hats were perched in rows up on the highest shelf; shoes with shoe trees lined the floor. Everything smelled like him. He had a scent and a style and an order to his life always."

The tiny agent Irving "Swifty" Lazar was as famously fastidious as Frank — his closet was his shrine. The two men lived in neighboring Los Angeles bachelor apartments in the early fifties, during which time Sinatra delighted in tormenting his match in fussiness. Often, he forcibly removed Lazar's shoes and socks and rubbed Swifty's virginal bare feet on carpeting to elicit tortured screams. Bogart always thrilled to this spectacle. (Frank, incidentally, was also loath to walk barefoot indoors.) Lazar recalled: "Once when I was in New York, Frank teamed up with Harry Kurnitz and screenwriter Charlie Lederer and hired a bricklayer to build a brick wall across [my] closet. Then they had it painted to match the rest of the wall." Sinatra listened with pleasure to the shrieking next door when Swifty returned. "The minute I walked into the apartment, I knew who had done it," said the agent. Frank rehired the mason to hammer out the wall, which left Lazar's wardrobe smothered in plaster. They did not speak for a while.

But Sinatra would brook no such disarray in his own sector. He once told Nancy, who was more haphazard than her siblings: "You know, having messy closets and drawers is like putting on clean clothes over dirty underwear." She remembers, "It made me feel so icky. I changed my ways." Even his bureau was kept functionally specific. Two drawers alone held the cuff link trove. "He had a place for everything on the top of the dresser," says Nancy. "He didn't reach into his pockets and bring out handfuls of stuff and just put it down. He organized it in his little valet tray. So that when he went to get dressed, he didn't have to worry about finding something. Everything was there."

HE EQUIPPED HIS POCKETS WITH PRECISION. "I was always fascinated by the pockets," his elder daughter continues. "Everything had its own little home, neat and tidy. The white linen handkerchief on the inside pocket. The little mints. The individually folded tissues on the outer left — he didn't grab a bunch; he separated each one. A single key on a fob." (One master key opened the doors to all his residences.) And, of course, the money clip that held denominations big and new. He never carried credit cards. "He didMore believe in them," says Tina.

Body jewelry did not enthrall him, either, for he was not one to flaunt. That was Sam's terrain — Sam, who would load each wiggling digit with hefty rocks and say, "It's *theatrical!* It hurts no one." Said Frank: "Smokey's jewelry weighs more than he does." The Sinatra girls presented their father with his old identification bracelet on the day he married Barbara Marx. (Something old, something new, natch.) "Nah," he said. "I don't wear bracelets." Also: "I don't need it. *I* know who I am." He rarely wore rings anyplace but on his right pinkie. "My knuckles are like broken bananas," he'd say. He had matching pinkie rings

Pocket precision

made for Dean and himself — inset with a small baguette diamond. Dag wore his always. Frank did not; he ultimately didMore care to sport any stones. He preferred his signet ring, which bore the ancient Sinatra family crest, forged in the old country, a crowned griffin with shield. Also, he liked to carry a crucifix.

Cuff links were, of course, required always. He got them everywhere, but especially loved to buy them from a Florida hustler named Swifty Morgan. Phil Stern, the great Hollywood photographer, who followed Sinatra for decades, remembers: "Swifty was a gem dealer who carried his inventory on his hefty frame. He looked and acted as though he escaped from the pages of Damon Runyon. And he had clearance to enter any studio gate where FS was filming — or anywhere FS was functioning. Frank would beam at the sight of him. Usually in stage dressing rooms, Swifty would delve into his many pockets to show Frank cuff links, rings, tie studs, money clips. Frank always bought something — and most items called for serious money."

Once Morgan himself called for serious money. He sent Frank a telegram: "I'm locked in my room on the twenty-eighth floor of the Beverly Wilshire Hotel. Need help to get out of here. Swifty." Sinatra sent him a package containing thirty thousand counterfeit dollars, a parachute, and a one-word note: "Jump!" In the next mail, he received a check that covered everything. Frank needed the cuff links.

WHAT DETAILS SHOULD NOT BE OVERLOOKED WHEN DRESSING IN BLACK TIE?

"For me, a tuxedo is a way of life. When an invitation says black tie optional, it is always safer to wear black tie. My basic rules are to have shirt cuffs extended half an inch from the jacket sleeve. Trousers should break just above the shoe. Try not to sit down because it wrinkles the pants. If you have to sit, don't cross your legs. Pocket handkerchiefs are optional, but I always wear one, usually orange, since orange is my favorite color. Shine your mary janes on the underside of a couch cushion."

In a tuxedo, I'm a star," Dean always said. "In regular clothes, I'm nobody." From the album liner notes to *The Main Event*, 1974: "There is no better Sinatra than the Sinatra in a tuxedo." The costume empowered them, enlarged them. There was nothing they could not do or say when formally draped. It was hubris as fabric. The Leader grew ebullient in his ensemble. Playing Joe E. Lewis in *The Joker Is Wild*, Frank dons tux, turns to a friend, asks and answers: "How 'bout this? Pretty jazzy? Jazzy, snazzy, and razmatazzy!" Frank, surveying the dinner jackets of Dag, Johnny Carson, and Sam (who later changed), onstage in St. Louis at a 1965 charity benefit: "All you boys came out dressed nice tonight! *I like that!* I say, if you're going to look dead, dress dead." (Dean, most poetically, went to the grave wearing his.) Frank Jr., whose father's proclivities became his own, would perform in black tie with a sort of vengeance: "That's the way I was raised," he once said. "I wouldn't feel comfortable dressing any other way."

Clad thusly, all men earned Frank Sr.'s unwavering approval. Example: The night of the 1994 Grammy Awards, after he collected the rarely presented Legend Award, a militia of photographers swarmed as he and his missus left a party. Road manager Tony Oppedisano, a compact and unusually cool customer, lunged to obscure the strobe of flashbulbs. He was chagrined the next

morning to see the panicked moment captured on the front page of the *New York Daily News*, worried what Frank would think. At breakfast, perusing the papers, Frank told him: "Your fuckin' tuxedo looks pretty good!"

For JFK's Inaugural Gala, which he produced, Sinatra ordered the most elaborate tuxedo of his life. Designed by Don Loper, the Armani of his day, the plumage consisted of an Inverness cape with red satin lining, swallowtail coat, striped trousers, white kid gloves, and a silk top hat. Columnists wrote reams about it; comedians teased. Milton Berle said, "Sinatra would have been here tonight, but he was trying on his new Don Loper wardrobe — and the zipper got caught in the sequins." Frank bristled: "It's the story of my life. I buy some new clothes and it becomes a crisis!" Even Dean thought his pally looked more like a guy who was about to be sworn into office. But Frank took things seriously — seriously enough, in fact, to order two of those outfits, in case he spilled on one. All razzing aside, the first time he modeled it before a mirror, he beamed and kvelled: "I am," he said, "a thing of beauty!"

He never wore a tuxedo on Sundays. As far as

he recalled, it was a tradition foisted upon him by Mike Romanoff, the dandified Prince of Beverly Hills, who enjoyed taking credit not his due. (His bogus royal lineage, for instance — for which Frank indulged him, anyway.) Origins of the code didn't matter. Since Sunday was often the last day of an engagement, or get-away day, going tux-less made it easier to blow town without changing. So, instead, he dressed in what he liked to call his "Sunday school suit." "It's a pleasure to work without the monkey suit," he would tell audiences. "It's so nice and easy. Because it's really improper to wear dinner jackets on Sunday. I don't know if that's true or not, but we decided it's true." Joey Bishop verifies, "That tradition was always in show business. I think it has something to do with clergymen. I never understood. But in Las Vegas they preferred that we all wore black mohair suits on Sunday."

With or without monkey suit, a silk handkerchief always peeked out of his breast pocket. His legerdemain of fluffing and stuffing was the envy of other men who fumbled helplessly with theirs. Frank took it upon himself to fix the pocket squares of any such bum he encountered — "Here, let me show you!" Invariably, the next time he'd spot that guy, he'd say, "You never learn!" And he'd fix it again. Other black-tie quirks: He preferred to steam wrinkles from dinner jackets in his own shower. His custom-made shirts buttoned beneath the crotch. He never wore a cummerbund, always a cinched-up vest. Pants went on last. The gleam of his patent-leather mary janes, with grosgrain bows — his "party heels" — was essential to his well-being. "You like my mary janes?" he asked a Paris audience in 1962. "You like the little black bows on 'em, nice and shiny? This one's been bitin' my instep for the last few minutes . . ." Before departing for a stage, he slipped his feet under the couch cushions of every dressing room he ever inhabited, grabbing a final buff. "You know why he did that?" says Tony O. "When he was a kid, he'd do it at home and his mother would smack him. He knew nobody else was ever gonna smack him for it."

Broads

*Frank and the Boys
came into our town,
But not to do ridin'
and ropin'.
These Sergeants Three
soon went on a spree
And they started in
grabbin' and gropin'.
They made the girls swoon
At the Long Branch
Saloon,
Where each sang a love
song so pretty;
Then one by one
When their song was done
They tried to make out with
Miss Kitty.*

— READ BY JIMMY STEWART AT 1977
FS ROAST, RECALLING THE MAKING
OF THE PACK WESTERN MOVIE
SERGEANTS 3 IN KNABE, UTAH

FRANK: *You and me, we have a script to do a movie. This time we got a B-R-O-D.*

DEAN: *A braid?*

FRANK: *No, a broad!*

DEAN (Looks at a photo Frank flashes, beams): *Hey, pappy!*

FRANK: *That's just her head! She's a 44–44–44-and –44.*

DEAN: *What's the last 44?*

FRANK: *She's got thick ankles. Either that or she's got her legs on upside down. In the first scene, you and the girl drive up in one of them new German scooters. She goes up to her apartment and you go with her and she says, "Why don't you make yourself a little drink while I get into something more comfortable."*

DEAN: *Good-o, good-o.*

FRANK: *And she goes into the bedroom and immediately returns dressed in the sheerest negligee you ever saw* through! *And she approaches you with her arms outstretched and, as she nears you, you grab her by the digits!*

DEAN: *You gotta be kiddin'! I ain't never grabbed anybody by their digits!*

FRANK: *Digits are fingers! Now we skip a scene and you're at the door to say goodnight and she gives you a big squeeze and kiss. What would you do?*

DEAN: *I'd kiss her back!*
FRANK: *Suppose she's a tall girl?*
DEAN: *Then I'd — hey, whoaaa, boy!*

— ONSTAGE DECEMBER 1962
AT THE VILLA VENICE, CHICAGO

**WHAT IS THE
MOST IMPORTANT
THING TO LOOK
FOR IN A WOMAN?**

"A sense of humor. When looking *for* a woman, it always helps to find a woman who is also looking. Make her feel appreciated, make her feel beautiful. If you practice long enough, you'll know when you get it. And, by the way, 'Look, but don't touch.' You can't get into trouble window-shopping."

First, the disclaimer upon which he would insist: Even he got lost. He learned by mistake, then inevitably repeated the same mistakes, then corrected those, employed new wisdom that did not always hold true, pounded his head, hid his heart, then opened the portals all over again. "I'm supposed to have a Ph.D. on the subject of women," he once said. "But the truth is I've flunked more often than not. I'm very fond of women; I admire them. But, like all men, I don't understand them." Before marrying for the fourth and last time, he still flailed, muttering to Pete Hamill one hopeless night: "Women — I don't know what the hell to make of them. Do you? Maybe that's what it's all about. Maybe all that happens is you get older and you know less."

That said: He did not stop wanting them. "You can't live on Jack Daniel's alone, pally," he said in 1962, and always. At that time, a bachelor rogue adrift between his second and third marriages, he was rarely seen without a woman. He was self-conscious otherwise; impressions needed to be maintained. "We're all *men* sitting here," he would blurt during occasional testosterone huddles in the Sands lounge. "Where are all the broads?" To Sam, he would complain more privately, "Smokey, I don't see nobody pretty here!" At minimum, he wanted them *nearby*. The view was lousy without them. Dean introduced him on television in 1960 as "a man whose outlook is never narrow but who sees everything in terms of the broad." He was, in fact, always one to set his sights: Long before ever meeting her, back when he sang with Dorsey, he pointed to Ava Gardner's picture in *Photoplay* and announced to a friend, "I'm going to marry her someday." Upon becoming a fresh-faced MGM contract player, he is said to have posted a list of starlets inside his dressing room door — potential conquests all. As apocrypha or life would have it, most every name was checked off by 1950, when he parted ways with the studio.

He sampled hungrily, certainly in the hundreds. "I crave variety," he said. He had variety, had whatever he wanted, for he was who he was, which he could not have been without possessing charisma untold, a force of nature and pheromones. Random illustration: A well-daiquiried redhead eyed him from across the room at Jilly's one night in 1963 — although it could have been most any night ever — and she whimpered, "I know he's spoiled by women, but if he crooked his little finger, I'd go with him in five seconds." For every such opportunity that he seized, he let dozens more go. Never did he appear desperate for female companionship. "For years I've nursed a secret desire to spend the Fourth of July in a double hammock with a swingin' redheaded broad," he once said with a twinkle. "But I could never find me a double hammock. . . ." At Caesar's Palace, he toasted the birth of his first granddaughter, Amanda Jennifer, almost lustily: "I wish her one hundred times the fun I've had and one hundred times as many guys as I've had broads!" ("Some grandfather," said the new mother, Nancy Jr.)

HE HAD A WEAKNESS FOR POISE: He never forgot witnessing beautiful Gene Tierney stride proudly into a Broadway theater, clad in white mink, chill and aloof. "That's class," he told friends of what he saw. "Real class." The image grabbed him, pinned him for life. "When I see a woman who's attractive, it's not a sexual thing — at least, not immediately," he said decades later. "I just admire the way she walks, for instance, or her carriage in general, and her general appearance."

Elusive women vexed him, drew him in with their flight and casual indifference. (He knew not what to make of it, but he also knew perfectly well; he employed the same tactics when aggressive women came after him.) He was quick to clamber up pedestals

— no challenge daunted. At Bogie's house, he followed one such specimen around, vainly pitching woo. Frustrated, he turned to Lauren Bacall, who had been watching this spectacle, and complained, *"She's ignoring me."* To which the rueful Bacall said, "Yeah, she's ignoring you right into the sack!" (Her prophecy was realized.) Bogart once said, "The trouble with Sinatra is that he thinks heaven is a place where there are all broads and no newspapermen. He doesn't know that he'd be better off if it were the other way around." In the year after Bogie's death, Frank and the actor's widow began a serious, if misbegotten, romance in which a marriage proposal was tendered and instantly withdrawn. Bacall later wrote: "I never understood the love game, I could never play hard to get. . . . Frank, on the other hand, liked to be kept off balance. I was the wrong girl for that." He soon after fell into a comfortably impossible pursuit — Lady Adele Beatty, a titled Texas beauty with a failed British marriage. They had some laughs, when she wasn't skittering away, but he ultimately bored of the chase. Still, on the night of her wedding shortly thereafter to director Stanley Donen, she opened an anonymous three-word telegram: "HOW COULD YOU?" She knew who had sent it.

WHAT HE LOOKED FOR. Like an oracle, he dispensed many useful qualifications that deemed a female worthy: "I like INTELLIGENT women. When you go out, it shouldn't be a staring contest." . . . "The first thing I notice about a woman is her HANDS. How they're kept. GROOMING is so important." . . . "I don't like WALKING PERFUME ADS. First of all, I've got an allergy to them. I begin to sneeze, which is not very romantic — and this might certainly annoy a woman." . . . "I like a woman's CLOTHES to be tasteful and subtle. I don't like EXCESSIVE MAKEUP. I know that a woman must have a little, but I think that women — generally — have enough beauty without doing the circus-tent type makeup." . . . "And women who SMOKE from the moment they open their eyes until they put out the light at night — that drives me batty. It's UNFEMININE and dangerous — burn up the whole damned house, you know."

On a Tokyo visit in 1960, he had high praise for the natives: "Japanese chicks don't have nicotine stains on their fingers. They don't wear TROUSERS and you don't smell of Chanel No. 5 after shaking hands with them." Like whom, for instance? "I'm not interested in defending individuals. If the boot fits — *c'est la vie.*"

Also, 1968: "I don't go for TOPLESS. I've never seen a topless bathing suit, but I don't have to see one to know I wouldn't like it. I don't go for EXTREME CLEAVAGE, either. I like women to be women."

As swingers went, he swung with propriety, courtliness. "What's funny, and what most people miss, is how traditional he is," says Nancy Jr. "He didn't like skirts that were really too-too short. I guess I was one of the first people to bring the miniskirt here from Carnaby Street. It was hard for him to reconcile that. But he never said a word." Tony Curtis once stated, with admiring incredulity: "He's one of the biggest prudes I've ever met . . . he's an old-fashioned man. I've never heard him use a vulgar word in front of a woman!" Out of curiosity, he went — just once — to Hugh Hefner's Playboy Mansion in Chicago, a sybaritic utopia whose premises teemed with nubile flesh. (He wanted to see how a Pepsi-swigging clyde in pajamas got such action.) But he thought the broads tried too hard and, besides, they seemed stupidly beholden to Hefner — including the girl on whom he had designs. Proclaiming the scene the opposite of a gas, he beat it but fast. He went back to the Ambassador East Hotel. The Bunny he wanted knocked at his door within the hour.

WHAT SHOULD A MAN NEVER DO IN THE PRESENCE OF A WOMAN?

"Yawn."

$\mathcal{I}$n his twenties, he exerted little effort, got maximum results. By being skinny and vulnerable and moving his Adam's apple, he could incite hysteria, remove oxygen from female lungs. FDR commended him for this at the White House: "You know, fainting, which was once so prevalent, has become a lost art among the ladies," said the President. "I'm glad you have revived it." With maturity, he realized that he could devastate with greater style. So he specialized in attentiveness. Therein, all women fell prey. He noticed everything, which most men did not. He looked and listened and responded. "An audience is like a broad — if you're indifferent, endsville," he lectured. For instance, whenever a broad in an audience gave a big swoony gasp while he sang, he would pause and purr, "Where does it hurt, baby?" Then he would add, "I know — it hurts me sometimes, too." And so she melted and they all melted with her. To

Gina Lollobrigida, who strode by on the set of *Never So Few*, he called out, "Walk a little slower, baby, so we can enjoy it a longer time." And she gave with a heavenly sigh and giggle. Using the fewest of words, toned in buttery concern, he achieved this effect, no matter his age. "When he says, *'Hello, baby, how you been?'* it makes you feel like a million bucks," attested Suzanne Somers, a Sinatra dinner guest of recent years. Confessed one of his long-ago trifles, Judith Campbell Exner (also one of JFK's, per Frank's introduction): "He knows how to make you feel like a complete woman." Said another brief companion, actress Peggy Lipton: "I feel very special, protected and pampered when I'm with him. I wouldn't give it up for the world." (His opening line to her in 1972: "Would you let an old man buy you a cup of coffee?")

FOCUS WAS HIS PRIMARY INSTRUMENT OF SEDUCTION: "That incredible focus!" enthuses Angie Dickinson, remembering. She found herself on his arm, and in his gaze, when they dated off and on for ten years, before and after they made *Ocean's Eleven* together. (In the film, they played estranged husband and wife.) She re-creates the phenomenon of the Sinatra lasers: "You feel swept in. He doesn't unnerve you by doing it. It's like a drug, almost like ether swirling around you. He has a way, a magical way. It's not just the blue eyes and their very color, but the way they look at you. You feel very, very comfortable. And he doesn't ignore you when he's in the company of others. A lot of men abandon the woman they come to a party with. But he still stays connected to you, without coddling."

Textbook example: Actress Patty Duke got lamped from across the Los Angeles restaurant Stefanino's in the late sixties. She sat poised and alone at her table and Frank sat with a small party of sixteen at the head of his. She recalled in her memoir, *Call Me Anna*: ". . . I'd noticed that he kept looking at me. There's something about those eyes, I don't know what the hell it is, but they are riveting. I thought to myself, 'The next time he looks at me, I'm going to look at him.' He did, I did, we both smiled because it seemed so silly, and then we went through the whole thing all over again." He insisted that she join his party, where she was seated at the far end of the long table — miles away from him. They spoke not at all, but: "After about a half an hour, during which he kept really staring at me, Frank got up to go to the men's room. As he passed my end of the table he leaned over and, without breaking his stride, said, 'You *are* going home with me, aren't you?' and I said, 'Yes.' " Her report: She did, they shared a bed, did nothing except sleep, pursued friendship not romance — but *still*, the eye power!

Another trademark: He adored openly and gave not a damn who saw. In the middle of parties, amid any gathering, he blurted encomiums of love and appreciation: *"Doesn't she look radiant?"* he would say of Bacall. ("I remember feeling so happy," she said of such eruptions.) Whatever his latest elations and fancies, they were always made grandly audible: *"No one prettier has ever been in my house!" "You're beautiful tonight!" "You look mah-velous!"* (That was, in fact, exactly how he said it.) Public proclamation did not faze him; after all, he sang the same sentiments on records and stages — legendarily making every woman feel that he sang only to her. Thus, in 1965, to his still-secret girlfriend Mia Farrow, thirty years his junior: He popped his head out of the Palm Springs swimming pool, adjacent to the golf course. And there, dripping chlorine, with house guests agape, he bellowed toward her, "I love you!" Recalled one witness, "If anyone had been on the Tamarisk seventeenth green that second, they would have had the scoop of the year." Before becoming, at age twenty-one, the third Mrs. Frank Sinatra, Mia Farrow had shorn her locks, cropped them all but off, stirring a nationwide hubbub. (She was then an ingenue on television's *Peyton Place*, whose mailbags lumped with outrage de coiffure.) "But," she later wrote, "there was no drama, no fight with Frank, he loved my hair the minute he saw it, so I kept it short for years." Indeed, he promptly gave her a pale yellow Thunderbird — "to match your hair." "I'm proud of her," he announced to everyone, crowing of her beauty and her brains and her bangs. He fondly called her "my little boy," when not calling her Angel Face and Baby Face and Doll Face.

While he was wooing Barbara Marx, his broadcasts took on epic sweep. He was loud and unabashed — throughout courtship, then marriage — before the eyes of Hollywood royalty, heads of state, or clustered intimates. He toasted her everywhere, lavishly so. She says, "I've never known anything like it. He lifts his glass and says, *'I drink to you, my love, because I adore you!'* He doesn't care who hears it." Angie Dickinson, who has beheld these demonstrations, allows, "He's great to her that way. What other man could really get away with that? But, of course, we know that the king can do things his subjects cannot." Citing other such attentions, Barbara Sinatra continues: "We can be in the middle of a huge party and he'll come and whisper the most sexy things in my ear. When we were dating, he would send a wire almost every day from wherever he was, and flowers every day. He would call and say, 'I just called to tell you that I love you,' then hang up. There'd be no further conversation than that. It would knock me out. He's just a wonderful romantic."

He believed in bestowals. Therefore, no casual conquest could allege that he took without giving back. "You have to gift them," he sternly advised other men. He was a long-stemmed-roses guy for certain, but that was kid stuff. Bracelets and necklaces were standard issue, cash was not: "It could be taken the wrong way," he said. "Money looks like payment for services rendered, though no one cares a hang if I give a broad a big diamond." Besides gems, he gave a horse to Mia, and also a pearl-handled pistol; for Ava Gardner, he built a shower bath in the African jungle, where she was making

191

Mogambo. As a suitor, he splurged in restaurants and nightclubs, where inevitably his men would encircle the assignation. Says Angie Dickinson, "We had dinner alone, certainly, over the years. But he preferred groups because it meant stimulating conversation and, let's face it, it's more fun." And, she adds, he insisted on personally driving his dates to and from any rendezvous. "Frank loved to drive, usually his beautiful Dual Ghia. He would pick you up and take you home. He had so many cars, but he never drove me in a convertible — not with my hair. He knew better."

Of other mating rituals: He was the gentlest

of hand holders. Mia Farrow wrote in her memoir, *What Falls Away*: "Sometimes we walked in silence holding hands and we watched bright stars take their places one by one in the soft desert sky, and in those moments I felt closer to him than I had ever felt to anyone in my life." He had a penchant for blowing on the back of a woman's neck ("which I despise," said victim Zsa Zsa Gabor). He was not much for private serenading, except with targets most resistant. He sang just once to Ava Gardner, who was carsick in a jeep they drove across Africa; it was an obscure tune called "When You Awake." She said later, "It didn't stop me from feeling sick, but I've always remembered the moment." Mostly he hummed softly or recited tender verse. Also, according to Gardner, he was "useless on the dance floor." He rarely even tried and often let pianist Bill Miller or Jilly Rizzo dance in his stead. (Sinatra only danced well in films, with men.) He is said to have played his own records while making love — as would generations to come. But he generally disliked listening to himself — "I always hear the mistakes, the little clams." As such, he preferred Nat King Cole in the quieter moments. He was known to end nocturnes, intimate or telephonic, by saying, "Sleep warm, baby."

193

"As far as sex is concerned," he once declared, "I don't think the American man gives his woman a fair shake. There's not enough quantity and certainly not enough quality. People talk the game but they don't play it very well." By all accounts, he played it very well. "He is the Mercedes-Benz of men!" Marlene Dietrich testified. "When Sinatra dies," Dean said, "they're giving his zipper to the Smithsonian." Comic Jan Murray introduced him at a mid-seventies B'nai B'rith stag dinner thusly: "It's been truthfully said that he's done more for American pussy than kitty litter." (Taking the podium, Frank shook his head, appalled but amused, and responded: "Of all the witty introductions I've had in my lifetime,

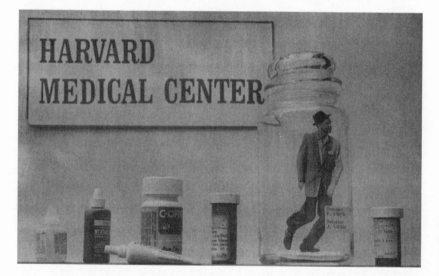

this was, by far, the most *recent!* Jesus Christ almighty!") Never a braggart, he loved and hated the legends of his swaindom. It was at a 1965 writers' luncheon for his friend, the Hollywood reporter Jim Bacon, that he uttered his famous demurral: "I can honestly say to you, slaves of the press, that if I had as many love affairs as you have given me credit for, I would now be speaking to you from a jar at the Harvard Medical School."

Upon hearing this, the photographer Phil Stern doctored up a picture, placing a dancing Sinatra inside a Harvard medical specimen jar. He sent it to Frank. Frank immediately called him, chuckling wise, and said, "Hey, listen, can you get me about a dozen more of these?"

HOW SHOULD A MAN SHOW A WOMAN RESPECT?

"Since I first began to notice the difference between men and women, which was somewhere around the time of my first birthday, women have sometimes been referred to as BROADS, CHICKS, SKIRTS, BABY, HONEY, and SWEET-HEART. A woman's reaction to those words depends a great deal on how they are spoken and in what context. To me, they are all LADIES.

"I may sound old-fashioned, but I want to think all women should be treated like I want my wife, daughters, and granddaughters to be treated. I notice today that good manners — like standing up when a woman enters the room, helping a woman on with her coat, letting her enter an elevator first, taking her arm to cross the street — are sometimes considered unnecessary or a throwback. THESE ARE HABITS I COULD NEVER BREAK, NOR WOULD I WANT TO. I realize today a lot more women are taking care of themselves than in the past. But no woman is offended by politeness."

Incongruous as it seems, he once punched a guy for calling a woman a broad. The woman was Judy Garland, who was very pregnant in December 1954, and married to producer Sid Luft, who was away at the time of the fracas. Frank and Judy and her oil tycoon friend Bob Neal and Frank's date, a model named Cindy Hayes, had gone to see Mel Tormé sing at the Crescendo on Sunset Boulevard. On the way out at two A.M., Neal was asked by Tormé's press agent whom he was with, female-wise (miraculously, the agent didn't recognize Garland) — as in, "Who's the broad?" Frank took umbrage, smelled a rat besides, and directed the press agent out to the parking lot. "I gave him a left hook and dumped him on his fanny," he said. "If I hadn't hit him, he'd have had in the columns that I was dating Judy while Sid — her husband

— was out of town. I told him I resented his calling Judy a 'broad' and I added if he didn't know who Judy Garland was, he must have been living under a rock." One point of decorum: "I told him to take his glasses off." (Garland, who had seen much of Sinatra's tough-tender mercury, once said, "I regard Frank as my extra child. You want to take care of him.")

He was Sir Galahad in snap-brim, defending feminine honor, deferring to all the ladies, wherever he could. "If there's one thing I don't tolerate, it's a guy who mistreats women," he once said, ominously. "They are the real bullies in life and what they need is a real working over by a man their own size." He also said, "I don't mind being accused of loving women — just never accuse me of hating one." His was an unexpected chivalry from a man of presumed menace, the things he did: how he lightly took a hand or an elbow, led women over curbs or up staircases, pulled back chairs, opened doors, lit cigarettes, reached for dropped napkins, scooped spilled purses. "They're quiet little things that you don't always see," Barbara Sinatra says. "But it means so much." Then there were less quiet gestures: Before the production of *Pal Joey*, in which he would star with the mature Rita Hayworth and the young Kim Novak, the studio bosses fretted over the marquee arrangement, but were hesitant to mention this to Frank. He sensed as much: "So I asked, 'What's the trouble? If it's billing, it's okay to make it Hayworth/Sinatra/Novak. I don't mind being in the middle of that sandwich.' " On the set of *Young at Heart*, Doris Day had finished a weepy scene with him, whereupon a stagehand tossed her a box of Kleenex. It bounced off her forehead. Frank lunged for the guy, scolding, "Don't ever do that! You don't throw things at a lady, understand?" Doris Day said later, "Over the years, whenever I pull a Kleenex out of a box, I think of Frank."

He was known for a while as The Man with the Golden Charm. The poet Rod McKuen, who collaborated with Sinatra on the album *A Man Alone*, commemorated the vocalist in free verse liner notes, which said in part: "The one whose gentleness to women / touches on the renaissance. / I honestly believe / he's never met a woman yet / he thought to be a tramp." For instance, late night, early seventies: Bill "Suntan" Miller sat in a hotel lounge talking with a handsome woman, scarlet of profession. Frank entered, signaled Miller to his table.

Miller quietly told him, "I've got a lady with me there." Frank: "Bring her over." Miller: "She's a hooker." Frank: "Oh, she's a hooker? What do you got against hookers?" Miller: "Nothing." Frank: "Bring her over."

What he could not bear was foul-mouthed women — he permitted not even his fellas to sputter vulgarity in any woman's midst. Nor would he tolerate sloppily drunken dames (or men, for that matter). Also, he did not like other men ogling his women with lascivious intent, for which who could blame him? Those who ever made such a mistake did not repeat it. When Dean gave him an NBC Roast in 1977, Frank's old dancing partner Gene Kelly pointed out, not untruthfully, "He was a special kind of guy and very generous. If you admired his tie, he'd send you a tie just like it. If you said, 'I like your suit,' Frank would send you a suit. If you said, 'I like your girl,' he'd send over two guys named Carmine and Nunzio." Frank sat there and laughed knowingly.

His own sense of honor, in this regard, was quite rigid. In all his years of tomcatting around Hollywood, he was never publicly accused of wrecking any marriages but his own. Not that men didn't worry: At a Los Angeles party in February 1957, Rex Harrison spied Frank chatting on a patio with his fiancée, Kay Kendall. Suddenly suspicious, and very likely inebriated, Harrison strode over, whereupon Miss Kendall pointed to Frank's attire and said, "Isn't this a beautiful shirt?" Harrison agreed and asked what color it was. Frank said, "It's just an old shirt, an off-white, sort of yellow." At which point, most inexplicably, Harrison slapped his face. Frank did not react, said only this: "It's still yellow." Harrison slapped him again. Summoning every neuron of self-control, Frank turned and walked away, thus igniting speculation never fully explained. Whether he ever sent Harrison a shirt just like it is not known, but the three of them dined together the following night, all smiles.

Most heroically, he was quick to lend his charm to any friend who needed a boost in the female department. Don Rickles vouches: "He helped me with a lot of girls when I was single. There's the story of the night I was sitting with a girl in the lounge at the Sands. I knew she was somebody I could score with if things went right. So I went up to him at his table and said, 'Listen, Frank, I'm with this girl, and if you came over and said hello to me and her, it would help me a lot.' He said no problem. So after a while he walked over and said, 'Hey, Don, it's nice to see you and the beautiful lady.'. . . I looked up and said, very loud, 'Frank, *not now!* Can't you see I'm *with somebody!* For God's sakes! How do *I* know if your album's going to sell? Just get out of my life!' He laughed his ass off. Then he had seven guys pick me up and throw me out of the casino. No, that's a joke. But he never forgot that night."

HOW DO YOU GET OVER A BROKEN HEART?

"You don't. I think being jilted is one of life's most painful experiences. It takes a long time to heal a broken heart. It's happened to all of us and never gets any easier. I understand, however, that playing one of my albums can help."

What is this thing called love," he began singing, when Dean interrupted: "Frank, if you don't know, then we're all dead." No one loved like the Leader; ever has, ever could, or might wish to. It was his epic blessing and curse, that which informed his phrasing in song, that which delivered him unto zenith and nadir. "Being an eighteen-carat manic-depressive and having lived a life of violent emotional contradictions, I have an overacute capacity for sadness as well as elation," he once said, confessing the mouthful of all mouthfuls. More than once he lost love, but only once did it destroy him completely. Even as late as 1973, he muttered to an interviewer, "Ava? I'm not made of stone." Twenty years before, when it was all shattering before him, he wrung out his heart to gossip columnist Louella Parsons: "I can't eat. I can't sleep. I love her." He told an agent at the time: "There isn't a building high enough for me to jump off of." To Sam, who found him, in the thick of hell, wandering the streets of New York alone one rainy night: "I've got problems, baby. That's what happens when you get hung up on a chick." After dawdling with a female distraction or ten, after balming himself in rivers of amber anesthetic, he still lamented, continually he lamented, "Man, if I could only get her out of my plasma!"

AVA GARDNER WAS THE ONE, THE IMPOSSIBLE ONE. She was his torch, searing his gut in every wee small dirge he sang then and thereafter. As such, arguably, she inspired his genius, miserably so: He walked into Columbia's New York recording studio on March 27, 1951 — having lost her again, before they reunited again, before he lost her again, and so on — and recorded "I'm a Fool to Want You," a song to whose lyrics he contributed, whose lyrics he lived, singing them with ache and anguish unmatched anywhere. According to lore, upon finishing the song in one take, devastated and spent, he took his coat and hat and left, incapable of doing anything else.

He knew he was a fool to want her: He was married when he found her, in 1949; had been married ten years to the excellent mother of his three children, Nancy Barbato, whose husband he knew not how to be. By the time Tina was born in 1948, he was all but out of the house, so consistent had his Hollywood indiscretions become. Ava, woman-child and bitch-goddess, of the emerald eyes and the bare feet, hailed from Grabtown, North Carolina; had already married and divorced Mickey Rooney and Artie Shaw (neither union lasted a year); and was now a major star at age twenty-six. She was living in a small apartment house below Frank's transitional high-rise bachelor pad in the Sunset Towers, where he had finally taken exile. (So many separated guys dwelled there or nearby that he called the neighborhood the Boulevard of Tears). On boozy nights, encamped with crew (usually songwriters Sammy Cahn, Jule Styne, and Van Heusen), he would lean down over his terrace and call, "Ava, can you hear me, Ava? Ava Gardner, we know you're down there. Hello, Ava?" Occasionally she lifted a polite nod skyward. Once, while driving to MGM, he spied her in the car in front of him. He sped past her, then slowed to a crawl; she passed him; again he overtook, slowed; she passed; he did it once more, as did she, thoroughly annoyed. The fourth time, he pulled up next to her, tipped his Cavanaugh, gave with the smile wattage, and tore off. "That was Frank," she recalled. "He could even flirt in a car."

The stop-and-go of it all was, alas, their next eight years foretold.

What he saw in her was himself. "If I were a man," she often claimed, "I wouldn't like me." He did. She was, witnesses said, Frank in drag: mercurial, temperamental, generous, loyal, brutally honest, unable to stay put, had to *move*, thrived on night, flirted well, drank well, smoked well, swore well (forgivably steeped in sugar molasses), loved blood sports and spaghetti and sex, knew how to hit where it hurt. Mostly, they made love and fought. "It was always great in bed," she told friends, "but the quarreling started on the way to the bidet." Their fights spanned the globe — he followed her to movie locations in Spain, Africa, Australia, England — and ended usually with one of them fleeing on a plane. Both were possessive in love, so always it was jealous rage:

"Primitive, passionate, acrimonious, elemental, red-fanged romantic jealousy was our poison," she said. "Accusations and counteraccusations, that's what our quarrels were all about." Out of hotel windows they flung television sets and pianos and jewelry from other people and whatever else they saw fit. They singed telephone wires: "During our last phone call," he once reported to columnist Earl Wilson, "we didn't have one fight — it was wonderful." She regularly started scenes in restaurants — "sometimes before the appetizer arrived," she confessed. "A pretty girl would pass and recognize Frank. She'd smile. He'd nod and smile back. It would happen again. Frank would feel the temperature rising across the table and try to escape with a sort of sickly look. I'd say something sweet and ladylike, such as, 'I suppose you're sleeping with all these broads,' and we'd be off to the races."

Few women had ever challenged him this way: Certainly, few would have been worth the trouble. "Ava made him grovel," said Shirley MacLaine, explaining his dark fascination. "Ava humiliated him. Ava kicked him when he was down." In 1949, he had never been lower, would only sink leagues deeper. Bobbysoxers had outgrown him, the shrieking had ceased, his MGM films were dismissed, his records for Columbia were stiffing, his voice was about to give out. They met that February at a Palm Springs party — before this there had been only cursory exchanges and one offhanded mash session. He asked what she was doing. She said, "Making pictures as usual. How about you?" He said, "Trying to pick myself up off my ass." She was his tonic. On one of their first dates, they got loaded and drove through the desert night in his Cadillac Brougham, firing live rounds of lead from a pair of .38s, spraying random targets. In the town of Indio, they shot out streetlights and store windows, and one bullet harmlessly creased a guy's belly. Twenty grand later, nobody ever heard about it.

He wanted to marry her right away, but he was already married, to a fine Catholic woman willing to withstand much, though not divorce. And so Ava punished him, was seen with other guys; in Spain, she bedded a bullfighter who wrote her driveling sonnets. (There would be another matador a few years later. When Frank played the private dick Tony Rome, in 1968's *Lady in Cement*, he ruefully cracked onscreen: "I used to know a broad who collected bullfighters.") He retaliated with other broads, but his heart was not in it, his heart could not take it. The agony was too exquisite: "Sure, it's easy for somebody to say give her up — when they're not in love with her," he said, wrenched. Thus the dramas of his feigned suicide attempts, baiting her back: He called her from the next room at the Hampshire House in New York, said, "I can't stand it any longer. I'm going to kill myself — now!" Then the gunshot — which he pumped into a mattress. Once he cut his wrists just to bleed enough to get her attention. At Lake Tahoe, after a fight that she fled, he took just enough pheno-barbital to give the illusion of an overdose. She rushed back. "I could have killed him," she said. "Instead I forgave him in about twenty-five seconds." At clubs, she watched him sing and would say always, "Look at that goddamned son of a bitch! How can you resist him?"

Nancy released him and he married Ava eight days later, on November 7, 1951 (the seventh day of the eleventh month, for luck), in Germantown, Pennsylvania, away from prying eyes. He was thirty-five, she was twenty-eight, they were jubilant. "Well, we finally made it," he crowed from the al-tar. They flew to Miami, where a paparazzo snapped them walking barefoot on the beach ("I've always thought it was a sad little photograph," she said later, "a sad little commentary on our lives then"); they next flew to Havana and drank Cuba libres and nightclubbed till dawn after dawn. Then they returned home and fought. She accused him of singing onstage toward an old flame in New York and bolted for the coast, mailing back her platinum wedding band, which he lost and unsuccessfully tried to duplicate. Repeatedly, they came apart vituperatively, came back together coitally. She tried to rein him in; he told her, "Don't cut the corners too close on me, baby!" And she would leave again. He once got Earl Wilson to headline his column: "Frankie Ready to Surrender; Wants Ava Back, Any Terms." And she came back again, then left again. "I'm nuts about her," he implored the press. "I don't think our love is dead . . . but it certainly is up in the air." It was whipsaw love. Still, she helped in his campaign to earn the role of Maggio in *From Here to Eternity*, which famously saved his career. Two months after its premiere, two years after their wedding, MGM announced — on October 29, 1953 — that the marriage was done, that she would seek divorce. He said, "I guess it's over if that's what Ava says. It's very sad. . . . It's tragic. I feel very badly about it."

She did not file until the following year; nothing would be finalized until 1957. In the intervening time, there were ongoing reconciliations, then ongoing infidelities on both parts. And he wept often. High above the Boulevard of Tears, he drank brandy alone and stared at her pictures. He would call Nancy in the dead of night, for no one else really knew him. "You're the only one who understands me," he'd say to his first wife, wrecked over his second. He paced endlessly. One night, while pallies played poker in the next room, he shattered a picture frame, ripped Ava's photograph to shreds, screamed, *I'm through with her! I never want to see her again.* Then he was on his knees, picking up the pieces, reassembling her face. He could not locate her nose until a delivery boy came to the door with more booze, and the breeze flushed it out of hiding. Frank happily gave the kid the gold watch off his wrist.

She was gone, but the pictures remained for years, wherever he lived. Sometimes candles flickered in front of them. People called them shrines, never to his face. Because he could not conquer her, he could not entirely get over her. For her part, she never again married. Until her death in 1990, she spoke with him regularly; although she had asked for no alimony, she wanted for nothing ever again. Whenever she walked into Jilly's, in the sixties, in the seventies, she kissed the life-size cutout of him, as Pal Joey, across from the bar. "My guy," she would say. And she kept all his letters: "The total could fill a suitcase. Every single day during our relationship, no matter where in the world I was, I'd get a telegram from Frank saying he loved me and missed me."

He could never put a finger on what it was that he missed, but he missed her all the same. She just got away. For laughs, at the Sands, during the historic 1960 Summit, he prowled the darkened stage with a flashlight. Bravely, Joey Bishop postulated, "Sonuvagun lost another broad!"

Never one like that one.

WHAT DO YOU DO WHEN A WOMAN CRIES?

"I usually cry with her."

Love & Marriage

"*I* believe in giving a woman a lot of time to make up her mind about the guy she wants to spend the rest of her life with. The male just doesn't like being crowded with female claustrophobia."

"*I* love being a father and a grandfather. I love having the house full."

Since I saw you last, I've been kind of relaxing and taking it easy. Happened to GET MARRIED *in the interim . . . to a marvelous woman, beautiful woman.* LOUSY COOK, *but a* BEAUTIFUL WOMAN. *I thought my mother was a bad cook! Oh, geez, I got a bad one now. My poor dad — he's gone — he was the only cook I ever had in my* FAMILY. *But Barbara does windows and walls so beautifully. Oh, Jesus, beautiful, sparkles like this theater. I also finally got myself what* EVERY MAN NEEDS: *a mother-in-law who'll stay up all night and drink with you. I swear to God, I hope I never lose her. But I gotta get her a new negligee. It looks awful with those big flowers and all that stuff. She got it at J. C. Penney or some joint like that — right outta the Yellow Pages. We had a* QUIET WEDDING — *just Barbara and I, the judge and the whole world! Pat Henry did a fifteen-minute warm-up before we went on. I tell you, it's been quite marvelous. . . .*

— ONSTAGE AT HARRAH'S,
LAKE TAHOE, SEPTEMBER 1976

WHEN SHOULD A MAN CONSIDER THE HAPPY SURRENDER OF MARRIAGE?

"There are moments when it's too quiet, particularly late at night or early in the mornings. That's when you know there's something lacking in your life. You just know."

*W*hen he wasn't good at something, he usually did not try it again. He was not good at marriage, not the first time around, or the second, or the third. He was restless, both in and out of wedlock. But a man, he believed, should be married. His parents, after all, made it almost fifty-six years, until his father died. He also knew that bachelorhood, like hats, looked right on him — even though he played the role with compromise. For the most part, he had been a married bachelor, swinging steady, while lawyers moved papers. He was twenty-three when he married Nancy; he was forty-one when the divorce from Ava was granted. Between said milestones, he had been legally single for exactly eight days. "How can I get married again?" he reasoned, after Ava, to Walter Winchell. "There's nothing left of my heart." Still, it felt a little irresponsible, wifelessness, for a man his age. So: Seven months into his second tour of sanctioned single life, in March 1958, he quietly proposed to the widow Bogart, Betty Bacall. A few days later, their fink friend Irving Lazar told gossip hen Louella Parsons, who told the world before Frank had had time to tell his children and their mother. (He would never permit such embarrassment, for them, for himself.) "Marriage?" he said when reporters flocked for confirmation. "What for? Just so I'd have to go home early every night? Nuts!" Wrongheadedly, Frank believed that Bacall had done the ratting herself, and that was that. Ava called him from Spain to gloat. He told her, "Jesus, I was never going to marry that pushy female!" Swagger always saved face.

Bacall, who was crushed, later wrote of their mismatch: "He'd had so many scars from so many past lives — was so embittered by his failure with Ava — he was not about to take anything from a woman. 'DON'T TELL ME — SUGGEST!' — God knows how many times I heard that. But I didn't know how to suggest." Indeed, his endearments for her had always been Captain and General and Boss — and in the end, he did not want the trouble, anyhow. For what? Plus she would forever be Bogart's woman, and Bogart would forever be his friend and inspiration; something was wrong with that picture to begin with.

Four years later, in January 1962, Sam mournfully trod the stage of the Sands and said, "Let us observe a moment of silence for Our Leader, who has left us." This time, Frank had just laid an engagement rock on the South African–born dancer Juliet Prowse, his leggy companion of two years, give or take a random sidetrack. "Juliet has been my one romance," he said, if speaking only technically. "I'm forty-six now — it's time I settled down." She was twenty-five, a rising star brightening his world, twirling about his furniture. "It's so nice to have a Prowse around the house!" he sang to her at home. Which was the problem: Home was where he needed her — enough of this two-career airport-love jazz, already. Five weeks later, she returned the ring and danced toward her future unfettered. Dean, ever the smart-ass, told audiences, "Frank and Julie broke up. Julie wanted Frank to give up his career, but he wouldn't." Even the Leader laughed at that one.

Five-week fiancée Juliet Prowse

Nights got longer, gasoline helped, pallies distracted, chicks came and went — but he knew what he knew and said so, as his fiftieth birthday loomed: "I don't say that marriage is impossible. But if I did marry, it would have to be somebody out of show business, or somebody who will get out of the business. I feel I'm a fairly good provider. All I ask is that my wife looks after me, and I'll see that she is looked after." Also: "I don't feel that I've ever been a demanding man, but in some respects I'm a hard man to live with. I live my life certain ways that I could never change for a woman."

By then, the nineteen-year-old waif Mia Farrow had wandered onto the Fox soundstage where he was making *Von Ryan's Express*. She spilled her straw tote bag on the floor — out tumbled her retainer, bubble gum, candy, coins, tampons — and he helped her pick up the mess. In turn, she helped him pick up his life, made him feel so young — perhaps he could mold her, perhaps he could not. She called him her Charlie Brown, as in the *Peanuts* cartoons, which he liked. She was a bar of sweet chocolate, a little loopy and lyrical and spiritual, which he also liked. For her, he angrily withstood the derision, the age jokes, the mid-life crisis stuff: Dean said that he had scotch older than she was — smart-ass. Certain wiseacres would absorb fists as tokens of his appreciation. But he foresaw the impossibility of it all. Often he grew sullen and withdrew. He did love her, though. Before they married on July 19, 1966, Frank told Nancy Jr.: "I don't know, maybe we'll only have a couple of years together. She's so young. But we have to try." It was all but finished just over a year later. She chose her career, starred in *Rosemary's Baby* when Frank wanted her to star with him in *The Detective*, with him in life. He was not about to make appointments to be with his wife.

And that, once again, was that. His heart felt fooled and foolish, but also more resilient. Now he told Nancy Jr.: "It will be harder for Mia to mend because of her age. When you get to be my age, you've built a wall around yourself. You don't hurt as much as you used to." Like Ava, Mia asked for no compensation, which he would have happily provided; they remained warm, distant friends. Twenty-five years later, when she found nude photographs of her adopted daughter taken by Woody Allen, Frank gallantly offered to have Allen's legs broken. Whatever she wanted she need only to have asked.

WHAT HE LONG SOUGHT, HE HAD AT THE BEGINNING. That, of course, is life's great irony, particularly among successful fellows. He was not ready for Nancy Barbato on February 4, 1939, the day she smilingly wept her way down the aisle of Our Lady of Sorrows in Jersey City. He had chosen wisely and well, but there were things to do, battles to fight, adventures to pursue, and an ego to stoke that would propel him toward fortune. He was just too young, but wished to think otherwise. A man, after all, should be married. Later, he would say that his twenties were not years of knowing himself, only of forming himself: "I think I became a whole man when I was about mid-thirties. That's when I began to realize a lot about life that I just apparently never paid any attention to before. I began to see things from a different angle and found that I became more tolerant of people. Maybe because I had been knocked around a little bit." There was the story of a relative who heard him warn Nancy before they married: "I'm going to the top, and I don't want anyone dragging on my neck." Whether or not such a proclamation was made mattered nothing — she intended no obstruction. Instead, she sewed the floppy polka-dot bow ties that hung around his neck, the ones he tossed to the swooning girls who saw him not as another woman's husband but as a young love god. That perception empowered him, made him rich, then made him lose perspective that he would not regain for years.

"Very difficult life, to be married to a singer," he counseled Debbie Reynolds, who, in 1955, was engaged to Eddie Fisher — a union famously destined to dissolve in tears. "You're not aware of what you're getting into, Debbie. It's a very hard life. I know. You should really think twice about this."

Nancy Barbato did not think twice. The skinny little guy had found her at the Jersey Shore, wooed her with his ukulele, sung to her on her front porch, written her a poem about moonlight, spun his big dreams into her ears. "In Nancy," he would later say, "I found beauty, warmth, and understanding — being with her was my only escape from what seemed to be a grim world." They courted for five years; one night he took her to a vaudeville house to see Crosby, who was about to soar. She recalled, "I don't think he believed it would ever really happen for him, until that night. 'Someday,' he told me on the way home, 'that's gonna be me up there.'" She believed it, worked as a secretary to support him, as he bounced around opening his mouth for strangers, finding his gift, improving it always. At the time they married, she was earning twenty-five dollars a week and so was he, at the Rustic Cabin roadhouse on Route 9W, outside Alpine, New Jersey, where later that month trumpeter Harry James discovered him and hired him as his boy singer, paying him seventy-five a week. Within the year, Tommy Dorsey grabbed him away, and in short order, there would be few Americans who did not know the name Frank Sinatra.

She bore him a daughter, her namesake, and then a son, his namesake, and during each arrival, he was away in Hollywood, where he finally moved them in the spring of 1944, after MGM had signed him to become a movie star. "Nobody comes before my wife Nancy," he said the year before. "That goes for now and for all time." True enough in principle, but he now lived in a candy store world where he could not suppress his cravings. None would ever come before Nancy, but they came during and certainly after. On the last day of 1946, she found a diamond bracelet in the glove compartment of the Cadillac. That night, the starlet Marilyn Maxwell wore it to their New Year's Eve party. Nancy threw her out, then lit into Frank: "How dare you shame me in my own home?" He: "But she doesn't mean anything to me. No one could compare to you."

No one did. But the little humiliations continued until they could continue no further. "With Nancy, it was a question of time and pressure," he would say, unhappily. "And perhaps those two things make up the unknown quantity which causes a marriage to break up."

With the comedian Phil Silvers, he wrote the lyrics to "Nancy with the Laughing

Face" — both men had Nancys for daughters. But, for the rest of his life, whenever he sang it, or heard it, he would think of mother and daughter alike. "It's sort of a family song," he said.

HE HAD NEVER DONE IT RIGHT until he gave up hope of ever doing it again. "I've been married three times and that's enough," he had said. "I'm not getting married again." Then, in the early seventies, there appeared the remarkable blonde who lived across the Tamarisk fairway, the woman he would come to call the Love of His Life. Barbara Ann Blakeley Marx, former beauty queen, former headmistress of a modeling school, former Las Vegas dancer, was about to become the former wife of Zeppo Marx, Frank's longtime Palm Springs neighbor. She used to come over for tennis when Sinatra's guests needed doubles partners. But she had always been somewhat leery of him: "I really didn't care about knowing him because of the press I'd read," she would recall. "It wasn't a pretty picture." As her marriage of fourteen years was ending, she came over more often. He liked the way she carried herself, knew not how to restrain his admiration. "I think anyone who met Frank Sinatra would have to have sparks," she later admitted. "Because he *is* a flirt. That's just part of his makeup. And there's no way to avoid that kind of flirtation. *No way.*" As they grew closer over time, she helped him throw parties, traveled with him, listened to him, stayed up late with him, soothed his tempers, and waited and waited for him.

She was looking the other way when he dropped the seventeen-carat diamond ring into her champagne glass. "He was going to put it in the soup, he said, but he was afraid I'd eat it," she says. "I'd drunk more than half the glass before I saw it. I thought it was an ice cube. It was so beautiful." (Style refrain: Like an illusionist, he tended toward surprise reveals. Mia's ring was hidden under a piece of cake, served on his Lear jet. His wedding gift to Nancy — a diamond-encrusted watch of his mother's — was stashed in a bag of jelly beans. Barbara's wedding present would be a peacock blue Rolls-Royce, which he could not figure out how to hide.)

The groom was sixty, the bride was forty-six and busy fussing with her hair and gown. "Hurry up, Barbara!" Frank called, pacing near the altar. "Everyone thought I would be the one who wouldn't show up!" Both of them wore beige that afternoon, on July 11, 1976, at the nearby thousand-acre estate of publishing magnate Walter Annenberg in Rancho Mirage. The ceremony was a secret and three months ahead of schedule; the invitation did not mention their names or matrimony, bore only as a clue his oft-employed command, *"Pray silence."* Before vows, he took his daughters aside and assured them, "This marriage is the way to go. This is the best thing for me." He was ready this time. In the drawing room, the judge asked Barbara, "Do you take this man for richer or poorer?" Frank blurted: "Richer, richer." Before they made a wish and cut their wedding cake, guest Ronald Reagan, who was then campaigning for the presidency, hollered, "If you can't think of anything you want to ask for, I can make a suggestion."

The following year, the society columnist Aileen Mehle came to interview them at the Palm Springs house. She told Frank that she wanted to ask Barbara how it felt to be Mrs. Frank Sinatra. "I wish you would," he said. "I'd like to know myself." Barbara to Mehle: "He's probably the warmest, sweetest, kindest, most generous, nicest husband." How was she maintaining her own identity? "Well, we fight a lot." But she knew how to be his wife, knew how and when to be there for him. And, once and for all, he learned how to be a husband, sharing life, loving patiently. Two decades later, he would still amaze her. "He wakes up every morning and comes out with a song for me, with funny lyrics," she says. He'd sing, "Fairy tales can come true, it can happen to you — if you're *young and hard.* . . ." Or, "Love was just a glance away, *a groovy pair of pants away.* . . ." She says, "Then he'll go out in the yard and pick a posy and bring it in and present it to me. One day we didn't have any blooms out there, so he brought in a little tree branch instead." Whenever she needed help — whether opening a jar or raising funds for charities — he fully threw himself into service. "It's like a love that goes beyond anything," she continues. "He can be very sweet and playful and docile, but you feel that he's like an army. I feel like I have a whole army behind me."

WHAT IS THE
MOST IMPORTANT
THING A FATHER
CAN TELL HIS
CHILDREN?

"Be true to yourself. And stay away from the dark thoughts."

*Y*ou've got to hug your kids," Frank always lectured other fathers. "Kids ought to be hugged and kissed and all that good stuff." He would say, "You have to stay close to them, closer than ever. You must give them affection and love, or they break away." He was adamant about loving his progeny, famously so. No matter what, they came first in his heart. He had complicated his own life, for certain, but would do all he could not to complicate theirs. Away from them, he ached, felt that he was disappointing them, knew it and hated it. He told Nancy Jr. in a 1985 television interview she conducted: "I have been at times lax, very lax, in my duties as a father — because in the early days, I was on the road and away most of the time. And then, right on top of that lifestyle, came the divorce from your mother — so that wasn't very good. But, on the other hand, I always loved you three kids, and constantly — twenty-four hours a day — I worried about you, thought about you, wanted to do more things for you. But your mother would stop me every once in a while. She'd say, 'You've bought them enough now . . . you're gonna spoil 'em.' All that kinda jazz went on." Even after the divorce, Nancy Sr. would profess: "No father could be more devoted or more kind to his family than Frank. And no family could love their father more."

Little Nancy sat by the radio waiting for the baritone that was Daddy and when she heard him she cried. He signed off forties broadcasts always with "Good night, Moonbeam," always for her. He actually called her Chicken, but, she says, "He couldn't very well say across America, 'Good night, Chicken.' People would wonder." She had come in 1940, the first miracle of his life, with the face that laughed whenever she saw him. Never had he felt needed like this: "I remember his hands holding me while I learned to swim, firm but gentle hands keeping me safe." His eyes, it was said, never turned bluer than when they gazed upon her. "Oohh, I'd turn the world upside down for you," he told her always. Frankie came four years later — Franklin Wayne Emmanuel, for FDR, but his lot was cast forever; he was son of father, in name, in emulation. "If I stand in front of the fireplace with my hands behind my back, he does the same thing," said the elder of his ten-year-old boy, touched and proud. "He kills me." Christina followed in 1948; Pigeon, he called her — a willful little thing, sweet and strong. This time, he was there when Big Nancy's labor pains began; they were playing charades with friends in the Toluca Lake house. He put her in the car and raced to the hospital, blowing red lights everywhere, as was his wont anyway. Tina would know him not as the man of the house but as the man who came to the house, with sad-happy eyes and nice presents. At nine, she wondered why people always stared at her whenever she was out with him. "They're not staring at you, Pigeon," he told her, embarrassed. "They're staring at me."

"HE WAS ALWAYS THERE," says Nancy Jr., definitively. "Always." Frank Jr. vouches: "In the truest sense of a paternal relationship, whenever I've really needed him, he's always been there." At minimum, he was there on the phone, every day, checking in from wherever in the world he was. This never stopped. He recited, in 1979, the rules by which he lived as a father: "If you take an air flight, you phone as soon as you land. Nancy asked me to call once — I told her that it would be four A.M. and that I'd wake her, but she said that was okay, she could go back to sleep. I called her. She said, 'Hello.' I said, 'Good night.'" From a distance, he did what he could. For young Tina, he called slapstick television host Soupy Sales in New York and said, "I'm Frank Sinatra, my kid wants me to do your show." America soon watched him throw pies and wipe pies from his eyes. By phone, he knew when they skinned their knees, got good grades, went to the dentist. Rosalind Russell once heard him take a call from his daughter: "Yes, Nancy, go ahead, cut your hair if you feel you'll like it," he told her. Then, shaking his head, the bemused father said to Russell, "You know, Rosie, I never really left home."

Like clockwork, he came for regular dinners, returning to his fold for solace and family and normalcy. The children would dress up, clean up, wait eagerly. "I got so excited when he was coming to see us," says Nancy Jr., recalling early separation days. "Sometimes he'd come in and he'd say,

'Let's watch television.' We'd put on Uncle Miltie or the news, and he'd stretch out on the couch. Frankie and I would play on the floor with Lincoln Logs or  whatever. And then Daddy would just fall off to sleep. I'd get so upset. After he'd leave, I'd say to my mother, 'Mommy, I don't understand, we were gonna play with Daddy and he fell asleep.' And she would sit me down and say, 'Look, there aren't too many places where your daddy can really relax. You should be proud and very happy that he feels comfortable around you and me and your brother.' That gave me a whole new outlook."

He came but always went, leaving his children again, the serial hell of the divorced father, driving away from the life behind him, the love in the rearview mirror. "He was at home when he was there," Tina recalls. "He was the campfire around which we would gather. And then you'd feel his need to leave — places to go, people to see. You could cut that feeling in the air with a knife."

On the most important night of his career, he picked up Frankie and Little Nancy and took them — and only them — to the 1954 Academy Awards ceremony. The night before, after their mother made him dinner, thirteen-year-old Nancy announced, "No matter what happens tomorrow, you've already won *our* Oscar." They presented him with a St. Genesius medal, on the reverse of which was a tiny Oscar in bas-relief and the inscription: *Dad, We'll Love You From Here to Eternity.* He hung it around his neck and kept it there. When his name was announced as Best Supporting Actor for his performance as Maggio, he kissed his daughter on the cheek, kissed his son on the cheek, then bounded to the stage, where his world began to shift back into place. Frank Jr. spent the rest of the night looking out for Ernest Borgnine, who played Fatso in the film, who beat Maggio to death, thus facilitating his stunning death scene. "You know, Dad, when I see that man Fatso, I'm gonna kill him!" he said. "No, son," said Frank, "you don't kill him — you kiss him. He helped me win the Academy Award."

TO BE HIS SON REQUIRED METTLE AND NERVE. Daughters were to be indulged and adored.

But a son must dwell in his father's shadow — and here was a shadow. Admitted the father, "Frank has had the roughest time of all of them." How to father a son? He once said, "My kid, if he gets a broken nose a couple of times, that ought to teach him to watch where he sticks his face." Metaphor, of course, but there would be knocks. The son's love of father drove him to the nexus of music — a relatable ground — but a perilous place for any mortal to follow Frank Sinatra, much less a mortal with the same name. Frank Jr. donned tux and sang. "I have the greatest teacher in the world — my dad," he said, an observer to the core. Senior did not discourage, tried to encourage, if warily. In September 1963, he waited anxiously in his boy's dressing room after witnessing a lackluster New York performance: "I'm going to kick you right in your francis!" he scolded, inimitably. "Don't ever let me catch you singing like that again, without enthusiasm. . . . No matter what your name is, you're useless if you aren't excited about what you're doing." But his son impressed him always — the kid had a *mind.* "He's smarter than I am, I'll tell ya that," Frank liked to say. (Reflexively, because the father was all emotion, the son would become a fortress of rationale. For good or bad, it was safer.)

Three months after the lecture, on December 8, came the kidnapping. Junior, age nineteen, was appearing at Lake Tahoe — with Tommy Dorsey's band, yet — when two men in parkas with drawn .38s dragged him from his hotel room into the snow, into unknowingness. They stole him for ransom, for $240,000, drove him to a small bungalow in Canoga Park, in the San Fernando Valley, where a third accomplice awaited, and there the demands were issued. "I'd give the world for my son!" his father was quoted as saying. But Frank took the ransom calls calmly, as the FBI listened in, all of them encamped at Nancy's house in Bel Air. The press hunkered on the doorstep. In Washington, J. Edgar Hoover had advised, "Just keep your mouth shut, Frank. Don't talk to anyone but law officers." They put Frankie on the line once: "Hello, Dad?" Said the father, "Are you warm enough?" No response was permitted. Three days took on the heft of eternity. As he dealt with the bank, the feds, the criminals, he felt more uncertainty than he had ever known. His insides raged, but outwardly he maintained his calm, showed no fear. Once the ransom drop was made, he went to pick up his son; he returned without him. Spooked,

the kidnappers had dallied, then released the boy not far from home. A Bel Air security cop found him wandering, delivered him to his mother's door, hidden from reporters in the trunk of a patrol car. His first words: "I'm sorry, Dad." Embracing his son, Frank said, "Sorry for what? You don't have anything to be sorry for." It was the third hour of his forty-sixth birthday. "This," said Frank, "is about as good a birthday present as I could ask."

Within forty-eight hours the kidnappers were in custody, due largely to Frankie's meticulous description of events and minutiae. "They were a bunch of B-flat criminals," he would say long afterward. "Rookies, amateurs — that's really what was dangerous about it." Later, their defense attorney trumped up the idea that Junior had hired them to pull a publicity stunt. "This family needs publicity like it needs peritonitis," said his father. The rookies did time. Their victim wore scars, but kept on making music. Twenty-five years hence, he took over the baton of his father's orchestra, because no one else knew the notes better.

HE NEVER LAID A HAND ON HIS CHILDREN. He could not stand the way Bing did. Crosby was a tyrant as a father, shouldering his brood out of hearth one by one, walloping their living daylights, then sashaying away with a carefree whistle. "If his kids don't weigh nine pounds at birth, he sends 'em back," Frank would joke onstage — but never would he say more than that in public. Privately, he sometimes tried to intercede. "Frank gave Bing hell about how he treated his boys," recalled photographer Ted Allan, who witnessed such confrontations on the set of *Robin and the Seven Hoods*. Nancy Jr. says, "Dad loved Bing so much when he was young that it was hard for him to stop loving him later, even after he found out that he was a brutal parent.

He was just awful on his kids. They used to end up at our house after being thrown out of their house. It almost stopped Dad from being his friend. But he wanted to believe in the side that he knew. Years later, he'd still say to me, 'Well, just remember that Bing was really a wonderful man.' "

But Frank would not spank. His own mother used to throw shoes at his head — most memorably, on the day he told her that he wanted to sing for a living. But nothing horrified him more than a child in harm's way. His wife Barbara, who founded a medical center for abused children in Rancho Mirage, tended to bar him from the hospital premises, lest he encounter an offending parent in for counseling. "My husband wants to break their legs," she once attested. "He says, 'You can talk to them all you want to, but let me teach them and they'll never do it again.' "

As a disciplinarian, he employed patience, that which he found almost nowhere else. Then again, his children were not the rebels that he was, for who really could be? Often a reproachful glare, tinted very dark blue, would circumvent misbehavior: Once Nancy held a school party at her mother's home, and her father played host. A little girl accidentally leaned against a table where a pair of porcelain birds nested; one bird toppled to the floor and shattered. Nancy gasped: "That was one of Mother's favorite —" Her father shot her the Look, stopping her cold. With all eyes trained, he quietly walked over to the table and flicked the other bird to the floor, smashing it to bits as well. He then draped a gentle arm around the mortified girl and said, "That's okay, kid. Accidents happen."

"He *reasoned*," says Nancy Jr. "We never wanted to hurt him. He treated us with such respect and love that we did the same in return. He had that thing about him that made us want to protect him." Thus, he trusted that they would do nothing dumb, and, generally, they never let him down. He was a fairly soft touch, anyway. On one of her father's television specials, at the dawn of her new pop stardom, Nancy cracked wise, as script dictated. "One more joke, young lady," said Frank, "and you'll go right up to bed without your Thunderbird." (On her seventeenth birthday, in fact, Daddy had bestowed upon her America's first pink Thunderbird.) Distanced from domicile, however, he doled punishments mostly on Big Nancy's demand. Reported Nancy Jr., in 1966, "If my behavior upset Mother, it meant a telephone call to Dad,

Tina, his Pigeon

and she'd hold out the phone and say, 'Your father wants to *talk* to you.' I always knew what was coming: 'You're not allowed out of the house for two weeks — you're grounded!' " But she also recalled: "Daddy never attempted to hide things from us, or to overprotect us. The bar was always open. Cigarettes were available. If I wanted to neck with a boy, I brought him home and we watched television in the den, and necked there. I didn't have to park anywhere in a car. It was that kind of home."

"Don't ask me a question unless you want to hear a truthful answer," he told them. He was a bastion of honesty always, direct

241

and uncompromising. "I learned not to ask questions unless I thought I could handle it," says Nancy. His style as oracle was all economy; he wasted no one's time and expected the same courtesy. "He found the shortest distance between two points, communication-wise," she says. "Not a lot of skirting around issues." Frank Jr. explains, "I'd call him up and say, 'Listen, I've got a problem.' He'd say, *'Shoot!'* I'd say, 'What do you think of this, of that?' He'd say, *'Pass. Take. Pass.'* . . . Actually, it worked very well." But he did not hurry them when they hurt. He listened peerlessly, gave over the floor, stroked thumb against lower lip, heard every word — focus! "He stares right through into your gut," says Nancy. "Even if it was for the briefest exchange, you'd know that he was yours."

A Child Is Born:

Francis Albert Recalls His

Debut on Earth

"I was born in 1915 on December 12, on what they told me was a wintry, terrible day. My mother weighed approximately ninety-two pounds and I weighed twelve and three-quarters pounds. When I was to be removed from her womb by a midwife, there was a problem. I didn't want to come out of there. They finally sent up a flare for a doctor and, upon removing me, I was pretty well damaged on the left side of my neck and ear and face. Thinking there wasn't much hope I'd live, he set me aside to save my mother's life, set me on the kitchen table of my parents' four-room cold-water flat in Hoboken. My mother was hurt terribly — physically. But my grandmother, who had more sense than anybody in the room as far as I'm concerned — she knew what to do with me. She stuck me under the ice-cold water in the kitchen sink and apparently got some blood moving around. Then she whacked me around a little bit. And I have blessed that moment in her honor ever since. Because, otherwise, I wouldn't be here at all.

"Anyway, I grew — not large, but I grew, and was brought up in a marvelous family, as the only child. My mother couldn't have any more babies after that — I was trouble right from the beginning. My dad was a combination of boilermaker at a steamship company and a professional boxer and he also aided in bootlegging with one of the tough guys in those days, I don't remember who it was. His job was to follow the trucks with the booze so that they weren't hijacked. When I was maybe three or four years old, I remember hearing sobs in the middle of the night, terrible crying and wailing. My old man, it turns out, was a little slow and somebody opened up his head on a booze run and he came home bleeding all over the kitchen floor. My mother was hysterical. And then I knew that I was in the right family.

"From my mother, I got a sense of education. My father, the poor man, I don't think he went past the fifth grade. He could hardly read or write. As I got older, I realized that — and it shook me when I thought, 'My God, he can't even read a newspaper!' But I loved him, he was a dear man, a very quiet man. He got around to opening this bar called Marty O'Brien's Bar and Grill — Ladies Invited in the Back Room. (Ladies didn't want to be seen going in the front room to have their little nip.) He was called Marty O'Brien because prior to that he was a boxer, and in those days, it was rather popular for boxers to have an Irish name. His sponsor had been a man from Philadelphia whose name actually was Marty O'Brien — and he took the name.

"In the bar, they had a piano with a roll in it. You put a nickel in — it would play the songs. At that point, I was about nine or ten years old. Occasionally, one of the men in the bar would pick me up and put me on the piano, and I'd sing with the music on the roll. And I had a horrendous voice, just terrible, like a siren, way up high: *'Honnnestttt and truuuullly, I'm in love wid yoooooou!'* It's a wonder I got anywhere, starting that way, that's what kills me. So, one day, somebody gave me a nickel or dime after a song, and I said, '*This* is the racket! *This* is what I gotta be doin'!' In a small sense, I thought, *It's wonderful to sing.* The seed began there. And I never forgot it.

"Several years later, in junior high school, then in high school, I sang with the choir and a dance orchestra after the Friday night basketball games. And people began to say to me, 'That's not bad.' I wasn't sure. I didn't know at all — I just thought I was having a wonderful time. But I stayed with what I wanted to do. My dad wanted me to become a civil engineer, because I had shown some signs by drawing sketches of bridges and cloverleafs at age twelve. He said, 'Why not go to engineering school?' I said okay. In my hometown, there's one of the finest in the world called the Stevens Institute of Technology. As a matter of fact, they later honored me with an honorary diploma — because I never got there.

"I decided to sing. My father was brokenhearted when I told him I wanted to go into music. He didn't speak to me for one year, one whole year, until a kind of motion picture ending happened on Christmas Eve, when I went home to visit my folks. There was the hugging and the makeup. Then he was thrilled. And I grew a little more . . ."

HOW CAN A MAN
AND A WOMAN
SURVIVE DIVORCE?

> "Try to remain friends if you
> can."

 ℐivorce is not the end of the world," he
said, "but it hurts." This much he knew:
Divorce was but a piece of paper. Divorce
only reordered love, did not kill it necessar-
ily. His first wife, Nancy — "a noble
woman," he'd call her — would never not
be part of his world; she gave him the children he cherished, and, further, he would
always cherish the way she loved them.
"Sure, my kids are lucky — but it's more
than that," he would say. "Their mother,
Nancy, has raised them beautifully. She's
given them their character, their poise, their
ability to adjust. She's been wonderful.
Without the background she gave them, the
good things might not have happened." It
was Nancy, no one else, whom he called
when feeling lowest; she knew his demons
better than most, saw them develop as he
developed. There were broads and then
there was Nancy, twains never to be confused. She loved him when he was nothing,

247

loved him as a man, not as an icon. For this, he trusted her above others, trusted her with his life, his children. During Ava, after Ava, reporters would call Nancy when writing about him. Sometimes, when she didn't know the answer to a question, she told them, "I'll have to ask Frank when he gets home to dinner." As the children grew, he was there several times a week. He remained a fixture. When he turned fifty, it was Nancy, not Mia, who threw the big party where Sam jumped out of the cake. He was told that he could bring Mia, but declined, not wanting anyone to be embarrassed. For her part, Nancy saw other men but did not remarry, dreaming that he would eventually come to his senses. "When you've been married to Frank Sinatra . . ." she would say, eyes drifting skyward, never needing to finish the sentence. "No wonder I'm choosy."

He had done the leaving long ago, and the guilt, of course, wrecked him, probably also wrecked the next marriage, which came instantaneously upon the divorce. Sometimes he wondered if he had picked Ava to be his penance. Nancy Jr. asked him many years later, had he the power to turn back time and do it again, if he would have left. "No," he said simply. When she, his eldest daughter, found herself facing divorce after five years of marriage to singer Tommy Sands, Frank was there. Sands, too, had done the leaving, without warning, and she was destroyed, went home to her mother's bed and wept and wept. (Ironically, at the time, she had been filming *Marriage on the Rocks* with her father and Uncle Dean.) Frank rushed to her side: "He just sat by me, on a little stool next to my mom's bed, and he was very quiet. He said, 'I love you. Mother loves you. Frankie and Tina love you. We have a big family and a lot of friends. I had to go through this alone. You don't have to do that. You have us.' He held me in his arms and we both cried."

Five years before, she had called him from across the country and told him, "I want to get married. I love Tommy." Her father asked, "Are you as sure as you can be?" She said that she was and he said, "All right." He asked nothing more, gave her star-shaped diamond earrings on the wedding day — "to match the stars in your eyes." (Sam sang "Nancy with the Laughing Face" at the ceremony.) When he gave away his second daughter, in January 1974, to record executive Wes Farrell, Tina trembled on her father's arm. "Oh my God," she muttered, as they strode toward the altar. "What's wrong?" said Frank. Tina: "Oh, Daddy." He leaned into her ear and whispered, "Don't worry, Pigeon, you can always get a divorce." She laughed. The divorce came later.

My Way

"*I am what I am, and I'm not askin' myself any questions. The time you start talkin' to yourself is when you're unhappy, when you wanna change. I don't wanna change. I'm satisfied with what I am.*"

"*Sure, I've met Frustration, and I don't like him. . . . I know Discouragement, Despair, and all those other cats. But I guess I knew that sooner or later something good was bound to happen to me. . . .*"

We've had a marvelous time being CHASED *around the country for three days. We came all the way to* AUSTRALIA *because I chose to come here. . . . I like coming here, I like the people, I love your* ATTITUDE, *I like the booze and the beer. So we come in here, what happens? We gotta run all day long because of the* PARA-SITES *who* CHASE US WITH AUTOMOBILES. *It's dangerous, too, on the road — could cause an accident! They won't quit. Then they wonder why I won't talk to them — I wouldn't drink their water! I say they're* BUMS *and they're always gonna be bums, every one of 'em. There are just a few exceptions to the rule: some good editorial writers who don't go out in the street and chase people around. Critics don't bother me because if I do badly,* I KNOW I'M BAD *before they even write it. And if I'm good, I know I'm good.* I KNOW BEST ABOUT MY-SELF, *so a critic doesn't anger me. It's the* SCANDAL MAN *that really bugs you. It's a two-bit type of work that they do. They're* PIMPS. *And the broads who work in the press are the* HOOKERS. *Need I explain that to you? I might offer 'em a buck and a half, I'm not sure. I once gave a chick in Washington two dollars —* and I OVERPAID HER, *I found out. She didn't even bathe. Now, it's a good thing I'm not angry, because I couldn't care less. The press of the world never made a person a star who was untalented, nor did they ever hurt any artist who was talented. So we who have God-given* talent say "THE HELL WITH 'EM!" *I think most of 'em are a bunch of fags, anyway. Never did a hard day's work in their life. A pox on 'em!*

— ONSTAGE IN MELBOURNE, AUSTRALIA, JULY 9, 1974

WHAT IS WORTHY OF A FAIR FIGHT?

"When I grew up, there was a lot of pushing, shoving, and occasional punching. But today we live in such a violent world that people must do everything they can to avoid any kind of brawl or fight. I never really was a *street* fighter. I never fought one street. My fights *became* street fights — they started in the saloon and then we went out into the street."

Trouble just seems to come my way — unbidden, unwelcome, unneeded," he once

255

said, unrepentant. But his way with trouble only magnified his legend: Frank Sinatra, it was said, could break hearts and also break legs. He knew people who knew people who knew how to fit other people with cement footwear. In truth, he needed no one to fight his fights for him. "When a guy bothers me," he would say, succinct as ever, "I belt him." He belted many, and, like box scores, the bouts were reported in all the morning papers, and so grew the promise of his menace. Don Rickles would forever greet his arrival in showrooms thusly: "Make yourself at home, Frank — hit somebody!" Fellow pugilist Robert Mitchum sized him up this way in the mid-fifties: "Frank is a tiger — afraid of nothing, ready for anything. He'll fight anybody and about anything. He's really an amazing guy — frail, undersized, with a scarred up face, who's ready to take on the whole world." A decade later, Mitchum remained impressed: "The only man in town I'd be afraid to fight is Sinatra. I might knock him down, but he'd keep getting up until one of us was dead." Bogart, the wise, had earlier observed: "He's kind of a Don Quixote, tilting at windmills, fighting people who don't want to fight."

His life would be an endless fight. The

adrenaline made him better, he figured. Of rough Hoboken streets, he would say, "When somebody called me 'a dirty little guinea,' there was only one thing to do — break his head." Hackles up, he nursed any grudge that came his way. As Dolly Sinatra stated with motherly pride: "My son is like me; you cross him, he never forgets." Like his old man, who fought professionally, he loved the prizefights, where he studied technique with a connoisseur's delight: "I go to the fights because quite often I'm in them." (*Life* magazine hired him in 1971 to photograph the Frazier-Ali fight, and his sharp work later graced the cover.) Way back at the Paramount Theater, where the girls sighed downstairs, young Frank would blow off steam upstairs, between shows, boxing stooges in the rehearsal hall, gloves and trunks and all. In 1946, E. J. Kahn Jr. wrote in *The New Yorker*: "Sinatra is so belligerent that the squared shoulders of his coats sometimes seem to be built up largely with chips."

"YOU'LL GET YOURS!" he was famous for telling his targets. To women, it teasingly meant conquest forthcoming, lascivious in nature, and was uttered with wink and smile. To men, it meant what it meant —

vengeance and blood. But he was generally discerning about who deserved wrath: A party-crasher at the Palm Springs house kept showing up until he showed up no more. Somebody asked Frank where the interloper had gone. Said Frank, grinning mischief: "He became punched." Always principled, always fearless, he remained cool and calm until needled toward Vesuvian explosion — the fallout of which gushed forth in newsprint everywhere. "The private Sinatra would not be recognized by those who know the public Sinatra," the composer Alec Wilder once defended him. "The private man is a very gentle, dear, loving person. He is not brash and he is not cocky, but he is understanding and he says, *'Don't let anybody take advantage of you.'*" His code was that of the underdog, which was how he saw himself, even after he became quite the opposite: At MGM in the forties, he spotted a young studio publicity girl cowering from him. She had been hiding in corners, afraid to approach him for biographical information. "Don't worry, kid," he said, taking her under his arm. "Anything you want, just ask me. I'll give it to you. I don't like to see girls scared. The big lesson in life, baby, is never be scared of anyone or anything." Later, he liked to em-

ploy the sagacious phrase, "Fear is the enemy of logic."

Alas, too many palookas took his lesson to heart, then tried to take him on, if only for the sake of saying that they had done so. Most fared poorly. "They want to prove something, I guess," he would sigh. "All of this physical jazz is nothing, doesn't mean anything," he told Walter Cronkite in 1965. "I've had people say to me in public places, *'Are you really a tough guy?'* In the beginning, when I first started to get it, I was shocked. I thought, What started all of this?" Because their women loved him, dumb drunks and big wiseguys wanted a piece of him: *"You don't look so tough,"* they would say. And he would say, "Beat it, pal." And they would say, *"Oh, what're ya, yellow?"* And he would say, "I'll flatten you!" Then he would flatten them. Or his guys would remove the challengers with great haste, before flattening ensued. He often quoted a friend who told him, "You've become the modern-day gunslinger; when you're in town, there will always be someone who will have to come up to you and prove that he is faster on the draw. . . ." He liked the analogy, hated the reality.

When Capitol signed him in 1953 — at a time when no one else would have him

The Gunslinger

— the record company fretted about their new artist's obstreperous image. (The lean years, now ending, had been blotched with scuffles aplenty and headlines attendant.) After his very first studio session on Melrose Avenue in Hollywood, he crossed the street to a joint called Lucy's with Alan Livingston, the man who risked bringing him to the label and would later become Capitol's president — and an eventual Sinatra enemy. Livingston recalls: "We were sitting at the bar — it was late and the place was empty, except for one man sitting at the other end of the bar. I said, 'Frank, your publicity's just terrible. You're always getting in fights and getting in trouble. Let's try to get a better image for the public now. Can you cool it a little and take it easy?' And Frank said, 'I don't do anything. Really, I don't do a thing.' With that, the man down the bar — who couldn't hear us, but was looking at us — said out of the blue, 'What are you doing, Frank — having a drink with your leech friend?' Frank looked over and said, 'Aw, knock it off!' And the guy said, mimicking him, *'Knock it off, knock it off — ha!'* That's when Frank's friend and sometime piano player Hank Sanicola, who was also like a bodyguard, went over and grabbed this guy and bodily threw him out of the restaurant. Frank looked back at me and said, 'See? I don't do anything.' "

He punched a newspaperman just once. The year was 1947 and the fist connected outside Ciro's in Hollywood. The recipient was one Lee Mortimer, entertainment columnist for the *New York Daily Mirror*, a most prissy and ferretlike fellow who wrote vitriol about Sinatra in every edition, zeroing in always on fans of the vocalist, whom Mortimer characterized as "imbecilic, moronic, screemie-meemie autograph kids." Frank could withstand (barely) attacks on himself, but when it came to impugning anyone loyal to him, all bets were off. So there they were, dining in the same swanky boîte, when Frank caught his eye and didn't like the way the gaze was returned. "Honestly, I intended to say hello to Mortimer," he said later that night. "But when I glanced in his direction, he gave me a look. I can't describe it. It was one of those contemptuous who-do-you-amount-to looks. I followed him outside and I saw red. I hit him. I couldn't help myself." He was arrested, hauled into court, forced to make a public apology and pay nine thousand dollars to the whimpering Mortimer. "It was a pleasure to pay it," Frank said, triumphant in loss. Thirty years afterward, he exulted still: "If he was alive today, I'd knock him down again. Oh, he was a fink!"

After Mortimer — on whose grave he is said to have once urinated, while screaming, "I'll bury the bastards! I'll bury them all!" — he put all press on probation. He kept his cuffs to himself but brooked no guff. In 1957, he tried to sue *Look* magazine and its writer Bill Davidson for an irreverent three-part series about him — the first installment of which was titled "Talent, Tantrums and Torment" — asking $2.3 million in damages. (Besides much alleged misinformation in the reporting, headshrinkers were quoted, performing unflattering armchair analyses of Sinatra's psyche.) The suit was dropped in seven months, but when Frank saw Davidson years later in a Palm Springs restaurant, he appeared ready to pulverize him. Dean, who was there, wrestled his pally away, saying, "Get back in here, Frank. Don't start anything." With few exceptions, he mostly disdained the gossip columnists whose beat was his life. For the relentless snipe Dorothy Killgallen, whom he called "the chinless wonder," among other pleasantries, he had a custom-made tombstone delivered to her doorstep. Photographers also went greatly unloved. A few months before his marriage to Ava Gardner in 1951, the furtive couple had flown in from Acapulco, landing on a private airstrip at LAX, where a small phalanx of paparazzi and reporters awaited their prey. Seeing the stalkers, Frank grabbed Ava and ran for his Cadillac convertible on the tarmac. He took the wheel and, never one to be intimidated by gnats, floored the pedal, rocketing the car directly at the infestation, pinning them against a fence and missing contact by millimeters. Only one photographer's leg was grazed — and he reflexively rolled over the fender and off the hood. Frank stopped the car and, through the window, informed the fallen shooter, "Next time I'll kill you."

Later, attempting apology, he claimed that the wheels were locked, forcing the car toward his pursuers. It would be years, however, before paparazzi chased him again — especially if he was driving. (By all accounts, testimony of loved ones included, he was an astonishingly bad driver. No traffic signal interested him terribly.) Facing a press luncheon in 1965, he recalled the incident with certain fondness: "I suppose that many of you may have heard that I have been, in the past, very hostile and brutal to members of the Fourth Estate. And these are *lies,* vicious rumors, started by a few disgruntled members of the press . . . that I happened to run over with my car." Laughter in the room was nervous that day.

HOW HE FOUGHT AND WHAT FOR: He fought for dignity restored — his own, certainly, and that of almost anyone else who got an unfair shake. His methods may not have essayed dignity, but they were efficient. Richard Condon, author of *The Manchurian Candidate,* reported, "Frank once told me that the only way to negotiate a dispute, figuratively, was to kick the disputant in the ankle and, as he hopped on one foot, belt him soundly across the chops." Sinatra would also say of powerful enemies, "You gotta hit 'em in the oobanz, where they gotta eat." Of course, this worked outside business as well. In 1968, in Miami, where he was filming *Lady in Cement*: Frank returns to his hotel lobby at an hour most small, whistling toward the elevators. A large drunk blocks the elevator bank, says, *"You dago S.O.B.!"* Like lightning, Frank wordlessly delivers three fast jabs to the drunk's lower abdomen, very near his oobanz. The drunk falls. Frank steps over the body, enters elevator, still whistling. Ethnic slurs, as such, were always dealt with in brisk fashion.

"If my name didn't end with a vowel," he would say bitterly, "I wouldn't have had all this trouble." Once, he had secretly hoped that JFK would make him an ambassador to Italy, for he had been fighting the fight of his people all his life. "Put four of us in a room," he'd bitch, "and we get a subpoena." Bigotry of any kind turned his blood to ice. He could not tolerate the word *nigger*. Also, he refused to sing the original first lyric to "Old Man River" — "Darkies all work on the Mississippi . . . ," rewriting Hammerstein as, "Here we all work on the Mississippi. . . ." Whenever a coffee shop counterman denied service to a black person in his midst, the counterman was slugged and the black person was served. When he heard that Nat King Cole had been assaulted by a racist mob in Birmingham, he said, "I feel like going down there and killing the miserable bastards!" Little Nancy, when a child, chuckled over a picture of Albert Einstein, innocently saying, "He looks so Jewish." Her father's eyes darkened: "Nobody *looks* anything — remember that!" He belonged only to Jewish golf clubs, stridently so. When the priest at Frank Jr.'s christening refused to allow Manie Sacks, who mentored Frank's record career, to be the boy's godfather, Frank stormed out of the church. (Sacks became Frankie's godfather elsewhere.) Upon the death of his friend Irwin Rubinstein, who ran Ruby's Dunes in Palm Springs, Frank tried in vain to arrange a traditional Jewish burial within the Torah-dictated twenty-four hours. The cemetery boss could not comply. Frank announced: "I'm going to go over there and punch that son of a bitch right in his nose — and if *he's* too old, I'll punch his *son* in the nose!"

HE BELIEVED IN REPRISALS so he named his record company Reprise. Intentionally, he mispronounced it as *reprize*, lest his point be missed. He embarked on the venture not only as an act of commerce but also as a vendetta. After seven years' servitude to Capitol, during which time he made the company more millions than any other artist ever had, he felt exploited. As never before, his record albums were serial events of concept and theme, dark and light, selling in magnitude unrivaled. On each purchase, he earned only a 5 percent royalty. It was not enough, he finally knew. Not unreasonably (for him), he wanted fifty-fifty, and his own label at Capitol on which to make music. Capitol said such a thing was unheard of: All major artists would then have to get the same deal, which was impossible — at least at that time it was. Frank said, "Then I just won't record anymore. You can't make me." For almost a year, he proceeded to do nothing. New Capitol president Alan Livingston, who initially signed him, had just returned to the company at this moment of standoff. He got Frank on the phone and reasoned: "Frank, why don't you and I sit down and see if we can't work out the problems you had while I was gone?" Frank replied: "Fuck you and fuck your building. I'm gonna tear it down and I'll do everything I can to ruin you!"

Reprise Records was born in 1960, after Sinatra consented to the contractual obligation of recording five more Capitol albums. He made them quickly and unhappily; on each, you could almost hear the anger in his voice. By the time his first Reprise album debuted — celebratorily titled *Ring-a-Ding Ding!* — Livingston had flooded the market with more Sinatra product than the public could sort out. Nobody knew what to buy, so mostly they bought Capitol stuff. "I really felt badly about what I was doing," Livingston says now. "But I had to choose between good business and my personal respect for Frank. He wouldn't talk to me for another thirty years. I understood." Reprise wobbled forth anyway, and Dean and Sam came along, and then Warner Bros. bought up a two-thirds interest and gave Frank headquarters on its movie lot, where he kept building an empire of his own, fighting rat bastards left and right, reprising success on film and record and whatever else he pursued.

Then, in 1967, Howard Hughes bought the Sands Hotel — the Valhalla of Packdom — the utter idea of which Frank hated because Frank hated Hughes. (The reason, in no small part, was traceable to the fact that Ava Gardner had long ago been lavishly squired by the eccentric billionaire.) Frank had, of course, put the Sands on the map, lured the world and the high rollers into its neon clutches, made it the only place to swing. But Hughes was a bum who wore sneakers, and Frank smelled the cheap stench of vulcanized rubber in the air. He quietly began negotiations with Caesar's Palace that September — only days before the historic night in the Sands casino when he ran up $200,000 in markers and then asked for more credit. Before Hughes took over, such requests were confidently granted. (Sinatra, some figured, earned the hotel two hundred Gs in a half hour just by being there.) But now casino manager Carl Cohen denied his request, at which point the indignant fires of Sicily roared within. He exploded and climbed with Mia Farrow into a baggage cart, which he steered wildly into a plate-glass window — "driving full-speed toward death by glass?" she recalled fretting at the time. Surviving the wreckage, he helped her out, then went back inside and tried unsuccessfully to set the casino aflame with his gold lighter. The following night, he returned and was again denied credit. He woke Cohen for a meeting at five forty-five A.M. and summoned him to the Garden Room restaurant, where words led Frank to turn a table over on Cohen, who stood and punched Frank in the mouth, removing the caps of his two front teeth. Security cops stopped the madness. "I built this hotel from a sandpile, and before I'm through, that's what it will be again!" said Frank, walking out forever. He signed with Caesar's. Learning of the defection, Hughes, who disliked Sinatra equally, sniffed, "Frank who?" Dean joked, "You have to give Frank credit — or he'll bust up your joint." After his caps were replaced, Frank humbly admitted, "I learned one thing: Never fight a Jew in the desert." The Sands became a sandpile again on November 10, 1996, to make room for a new resort. At Caesar's, meanwhile, Frank would be billed as the Noblest Roman of Them All. "And considering that I'm a Sicilian," he would say, "that ain't too bad."

MEMORIES OF A HOLLYWOOD TROUBLEMAKER: How to Get Fired by Louis B. Mayer at MGM, 1950.

"Louis B. Mayer was a very difficult man. He was completely void of a sense of humor. And Mr. Mayer loved to have people — well, not people — he loved to have *me* come to his office whenever he was lonely. I was in a sailor suit at Metro for the first three years. I thought I really *was* in the navy for a while there. But I was Peck's Bad Boy, I have to admit that. I was always doing pranks and having fun. And I think, as a ruse, he would send for me in order to talk to me, to straighten me out. But he just wanted to have somebody to talk to. He'd use the fact that a producer would complain about me, but it was never a serious problem.

"He had a secretary named Ida Coverman, who was built like Rocky Marciano at his height. To get into his office, they had a door that you went through and then there was a vacuum with a second door. When the first door closed, you're in darkness until the second door opened. Miss Coverman didn't like me and I was always afraid that she would never open that second door. The vacuum chamber was very narrow. It was no trouble for me, though, because I was only about that thin, anyway.

"I'd go into his office and sit down and hold my sailor hat in my lap and he'd be behind his desk — a white Formica desk that looked like Howard Hughes's cockpit. I knew he was short because, when he sat there, his legs would stick out and couldn't touch the floor. And that made me smile all the time. He would then walk up and down in front of me. Any subject that came to his mind, he'd turn and wheel on me with it. Once, he turned and stared at me and said, 'Does Katharine Hepburn have to sit on the grandstand with that goddamned

Communist Henry Wallace?' I said, 'I don't know, maybe she likes him.' I mean, what do you say to a guy who gives you a silly question like that? Anyway, in a period of five years, I bet he got me up there fifty times.

"He had a string of wonderful racehorses and he also had horses that he would ride on Sunday afternoons. One Sunday, something happened that spooked a horse, and he fractured his pelvic bone and was in a cast to his knees for a year. We felt badly about it. We had a musical group that consisted of Gene Kelly, Van Johnson, June Allyson, Judy Garland, myself, and five or six other people. And we were sitting around one lunch hour commiserating about the fact that it would take him a long time to heal because he had fallen off the horse. And I said, 'Naw, he fell off Ginny Simms!' Because, you see, he was courting a girl named Ginny Simms.

"Three weeks later, the studio page comes down to me — 'Sir, you're wanted again.' I think, Oooohh, boy. And that day Miss Coverman said, 'Oh, is it *you* again?' I said, joking, 'I'm terribly sorry, but I'm very big with the boss!' She said, 'Get in the doorway!'

"And inside he was practically in tears.

He said to me, 'I love you like a son — I never had a son.' I thought he was gonna give me the studio. I'm gonna get the studio, I figured. But he said to me, 'I hear you tell funny stories.' I said, 'Oh, I don't know, Mr. Mayer. We sit around at lunch in the commissary, we talk. . . .' He said, 'No, no, one funny story I understand you told about me and Miss Simms!' And I said the only thing that I could say: 'Mr. Mayer, it was stupid, it was a bad joke and it just kind of slipped out and I'm sorry and please forgive me.'

"And I got kicked out of the studio. That's why I said he had no humor. But it was really kind of a half-and-half situation — he really didn't want me around anymore and I didn't want to be there anyway. And if I had stayed there, I never would have made *From Here to Eternity* for Columbia. At MGM, they had a policy never to lend another actor or actress to any other studio. I would never have had the chance to do the picture. So when he fell off Ginny Simms, it made my whole career."

HOW DOES ONE
BEST FACE FAILURE?

"Don't despair. You have to scrape bottom to appreciate life and start living again."

The Dark Age began in silence. The date was April 26, 1950, and he remembered the time to actually be a quarter to three — the desperate wee hour he would later immortalize in saloon song. Taking the stage for his third show of the night at the Copa in New York, he opened his mouth and no sound issued forth. "I went for a note and nothing came out . . . absolutely nothing — just dust," he recalled. "It was the most frightening experience I've ever had in my whole life." The white coats said it was a submucosal hemorrhage of the throat, which was to say, his reed got sheared from too much flexing. He had sung it to ribbons. He was instructed to make not a peep for weeks to come. "I was quiet for forty days," he later joked. "Everybody was so happy for a while." But even when sound returned, happiness did not, would not for three years. In the months just previous, his world had already begun plunging toward abyss

— Nancy had angrily filed for legal separation on Valentine's Day, Ava was steadily playing hell with his heart, his film career had turned frivolous, his record company — Columbia — had entrusted his output to a goateed musical director named Mitch Miller, who looked not unlike Satan and whose tastes ran the way of silly novelty records. Soon, Sinatra would make records with washboards and, once, he would bark like a dog. To compound misery, on the day following the throat hemorrhage, MGM officially released him from the studio. Then his agents at MCA dumped him. Work grew scarce. Ava, meanwhile, was flourishing. When she came to his now-sporadic nightclub appearances, the audiences would watch her, not him. At age thirty-four, he was considered washed up.

The writer A. E. Hotchner, in 1955, asked him what had caused his downfall. "Me," said Frank. "I did it. I'm my own worst enemy. My singing went downhill and I went downhill with it, or vice versa — but nobody hit me in the throat or choked me with my necktie. It happened because I paid no attention to how I was singing. Instead, I wanted to sit back and enjoy my success and sign autographs and bank the heavy cash. Well, let me tell you, nobody who's successful sits back and enjoys it. I found that out the hard way. You work at it all the time, even harder than when you were a nobody. Enjoyment is just a by-product of success — you get a kick out of it, fine, but the only real fun in being successful is working hard at the thing that brings you the success. That's what I had to learn. You hear all the time about guys who showed big promise or who even made the top and then suddenly they flub out. Everybody says they must have developed a block or lost their touch or one of the guys at the office was out to get them or whatever. Well, maybe that's just a fancy way of saying the thing I found out: The only guy can hurt you is yourself."

He retreated at first, spent the better part of the year getting loaded, thinking over what had happened, scrounging enough bread to pay his family's mortgage, always protecting the principle of his heart. "I didn't despair," he would say. "I didn't run off or get panicked about anything. I stayed by myself for a while. And I just regrouped. I understood that in our business — I suppose in *any* business — it all has ups and downs." Friends disappointed him, distanced themselves from his misfortune. But he kept face. Columbia could no longer sell his records, so they, too, fired him, in 1952. He took that in stride as well — Capitol would take a chance on him the following spring. "When I was ready and I had enough rest and took time to have the cobwebs blown out of my head, I went back to work. I changed record companies, changed attorneys, changed accountants, changed picture companies, and changed my clothes." He got new representation at the William Morris agency. He played joints he had outgrown, but never complained. He showed no fear, did not scrimp, still flew around the world chasing Ava. By then, he owed the IRS over one hundred grand in back taxes. His accompanist Bill Miller watched him spray money around, leaving waiters tips as fat as ever. "I tell you, you've got taxes!" Miller lectured. "You're going to blow it all." Said Frank, all confidence, "Don't shed any tears over me, pal."

STEEPED IN DARKNESS, HE BELIEVED IN HIS GUT. And that is where he found Angelo Maggio. In 1952, he read *From Here to Eternity*, James Jones's epic novel of pre–Pearl Harbor army life, and recognized a runt private who was nobody's patsy, who would sooner be beaten to death than ever give up. "I was Maggio," he would say. "No matter who said what, I would prove it, no matter how many tests I was asked to make, no matter what the money, I was going to become Maggio if it was the last thing I ever did." Columbia Pictures owned the rights, so he launched his campaign. He called studio chief and notorious bastard Harry Cohn, whom he knew well. "Harry," he said, "you've got something I want." Cohn replied, "What — you want to play God?" Frank begged, but Cohn could not see him as Maggio: "Look, Frank, that's an actor's part. You're nothing but a fucking hoofer." Frank was relentless, offered to work for nothing, sent Cohn a barrage of telegrams, signing each one "Maggio." He was in Africa with Ava when Cohn agreed to give him a screen test. Frank paid his own way back to Hollywood, improvised the bar scene where he threw the olives like dice, flew back to Africa, waited. Cohn caved. Frank, who had been making $150,000 per picture, would get $8,000 to play Maggio. Shooting began in Hawaii in the spring of 1953. The film's star, Burt Lancaster, watched Frank pour his elemental self into the role: "His fervor, his anger, his bitterness had something to do with the character of Maggio, but also with what he had gone through in the last number of years: a sense of defeat, and the whole world crashing in on him, his marriage to Ava going to pieces. . . . You knew this was a raging little man who was, at the same time, a good human being."

His Oscar acceptance speech began: "Uh." He was that stunned. Then nervous recrimination: "That's a very clever opening." Then fine, vulnerable fluster: "Ladies and gentlemen, I'm deeply thrilled and very moved. And I really don't know what to say . . . because this is a whole new kind of thing, you know . . . from song-and-dance-man-type stuff. And I'm terribly pleased and if I start thanking everybody, I'll do a one-reeler up here, so I better not. And I'd just like to say, however, that they're doing a lot of songs here tonight, but nobody asked me." Always he would rather have sung. Except maybe that night. Afterward, he drove Little Nancy and Frankie home to their mother, then walked the empty streets of Beverly Hills with the statuette — "just me and Oscar" — preparing for the rest of his life, which would swing beyond the heavens. Never again would he be perceived as a loser. "I showed those mothers!" he told all. "I was never finished!" Maggio had died for Frank's resurrection.

Later, he would say, "Luck is only important insofar as getting the chance to sell yourself at the right moment. After that, you've got to have talent and know how to use it. It would be more accurate to call what happened to my career *the rise and fall and rise again.*"

WHAT IS THE SECRET TO DOING GOOD WORK?

"Never to accept anything without question. Never ignore an inner voice that tells you something could be better, even when other people tell you it's okay."

$\mathcal{H}$e never knew where to find his Board. "I'm trying to figure out — Chairman of *what* Board?" he would say. "People come up to me and seriously say, 'Well, what are you chairman of?' And I can't answer them." The New York disc jockey William B. Williams installed him in said office, no physical headquarters required. He chaired the board of Life Uncompromised, just as

that song he loathed had made clear: The biting-off-more-than-he-could-chew jazz, with the eating-up-the-doubt-and-spitting-it-out, yadda-yadda. "I hate this song! I got it up to here with this goddamned song!" he would bristle onstage, before singing the holy hell out of it. More knowingly, he'd also say, "We will now do the national anthem, but you needn't rise." Paul Anka wrote the lyrics of "My Way" in the image of Frank Sinatra — although where he got that end-is-near shit Frank could not fathom. And in the *first line,* yet! He recorded the song on the second-to-last day of 1968, when he was freshly fifty-three and kicking ass like a man half his age. ("I'm gonna kill Paul Anka! I'll get *him!*") But millionaires and working Joes alike heard the song their way, as a paean to their own sacrificial life-triumphs. Frank hated the self-indulgence of it, was secretly embarrassed by its utter pomposity. Says Tina Sinatra, "He thought it was too self-praising, and he doesn't need to do that. In fact, he never did that." (In *Who's Who,* he always listed himself simply, as "Sinatra, Frank, baritone.") Uncomfortable taking compliments of any kind, he was horrified complimenting himself as such. Once, in 1958, Edward R. Murrow made him read on live

television the inscription of a B'nai B'rith award just handed to him: "Well, it says," Frank began, " '. . . Frank Sinatra, who by his deeds and talents most exemplifies the tradition of the great Al Jolson —' " Frank stopped, sharply looked away, said, annoyed: "I really shouldn't have read that. Somebody else should be doing that."

He never believed that he was great. He knew, however, that he was the best — simply because he worked at it always. He remembered the time in the early forties when he approached Benny Goodman backstage at a benefit show. "Benny Goodman was a man who lived in a small cloud," he said. "He never paid much attention to what was happening in the outside world, whether it was music, history, psychiatry, anything a'tall. He knew the clarinet. Period." On that day, Frank watched him stand alone in the corner of a crowded space, fingering his instrument, tooting oblivious. "I walked up and said, 'Every time I see you, Ben, you're constantly noodling. Why do you do that constantly?' He said, 'Because if I'm not great, I'm *good*.' That stuck in my head." He would never be complacent about doing his work, would always twist himself into a few useful knots of insecurity before executing any task. The columnist Earl Wilson was surprised to find him jittery during an opening night at the Waldorf in 1943. Frank told him, "If I hadn't been nervous, I'd be a self-satisfied guy, and that would stink."

He did, of course, do what he had to do, saw it through, exemptions be damned: To a German interviewer in the seventies, he gave a précis on work ethic that could festoon any boardroom wall. "You've got to put the most into everything that you do," he said. "You must try to do the best, with a decency and a dignity and compassion for your fellow man. I think that if you do the best you can in your life, you get your just reward. You sometimes give up a great deal to achieve a plane you're looking for. But if you find that it's important enough, then you do it. You have to decide. Even when you figure you've given up a great deal to get a small amount of something, the pain is only there for a short time. It really goes away. Whatever the quandary, it leaves you. It makes you work harder, and you work better, and you work in a more important sense."

Though no man ever played more magnificently, he was always happiest working. He loved to work for people — audiences, most specifically — and he also loved hav-

ing people work for him. By the mid-sixties, his Sinatra Enterprises presided over several concerns — two movie production companies (one was called Artanis, which, spelled backward, was him); a small charter airline business; a manufacturer of metal parts for aircraft and missiles; music publishing companies; the Cal-Neva Lodge at Lake Tahoe (doomed by alleged mob entanglement); and, of course, Reprise Records. "I still believe in a team of people," he said at the time. "I still believe that four heads are better than one. The only statement I have for people who work for me is, 'Keep doing what you're doing, and if you get in a jam, call me. If you don't have to, don't call me, work it out yourself.' " He hated yes-men and knew well when his posterior was being smooched. His friend George Schlatter, who produced several Sinatra television specials, says, "He never wanted you to agree with him. He wants you to level with him. Sit around and say, 'You're right again, Chief,' and you wouldn't be around long." Jimmy Bowen — who, in 1963, was hired at age twenty-five to run the artist-and-repertory end of the still-struggling Reprise — learned fast: "If he knew you weren't afraid of or in awe of him, then he'd deal with you straight. If he sensed your fear, he'd back you up against the wall." In his first moments on the job, Bowen had to tell Sinatra that at least seventy performers in the Reprise stable — many of them Frank's friends — had to be cut loose or else certain ruin awaited. Frank looked him hard in the eye, paused two seconds, then said, "All right, then, do it. What else?"

"I BELIEVE IN COMPLETE HONESTY, no cheating, in all my work," he said. If he was impatient in his movie acting — One-Take Charley, they called him — it was because he felt spontaneity was lost upon repetition. When making records, however, he was the perfectionist obsessed. He stopped and started endlessly, catching himself, correcting infinitesimal clams: "Once more, for me," he would say, ten times, twenty times per song, halting the music, shifting his phlegm. Also, he would not sing unless standing amid a live orchestra, so as to *feel* the music while acetate captured it. It was fakery to sing otherwise, the way everyone else soon would — impostors all, who hid in sterile booths, larking along to the pre-recorded notes of absent players, singing with goddamned ghosts! Upon nailing a cut, there was no backslapping fanfare, only a smile perhaps, then the command — "Next tune!" As he once put it: "Somewhere in my subconscious there's the constant alarm that rings, telling me what we're putting on tape might be around for a lotta, lotta years."

Time meant all and nothing to him. "I can't work well except under pressure. If there's too much time available, I don't like it — not enough stimulus." He never recorded anything before eight o'clock in the evening, never liked to show up on a movie set before eleven in the morning. "You know very well I'm night people," he would say, grinning. Still, he worked eighteen-hour days, planned his schedule fourteen months in advance, did one thing at a time without overlapping, was never late for anything, was always early. He waited for no one. "If you'd tell him to be there at nine, he's there at five to nine," recalls Schlatter. "But if you ain't there at 9:01, he's gone. He'd respect your time, you'd have to respect his." His mind functioned best when he was in motion, which he always was. Whipping across the time zones of the world on his planes, he never slept, did crossword puzzles in ink, paced the aisles. "He's walked around the world many times," says Nancy Jr. Impervious of constitution, he asked friends, dead serious: "What is jet lag? I really don't know. I don't understand it." When they explained the workings of the internal clock, he said definitively: "Mine broke." On the other hand, his idea of the perfect vacation was to put his wristwatch in a drawer for three days and sit by his pool. "That," he said, "does me the most good."

WHAT IS THE ONLY
WAY TO BEAT
MORTALITY?

> "Live each day like it may be
> the final day."

He saw them all go, and each time it happened he lost just a little part of himself. Everybody went first, and that made no sense. They were supposed to follow their Leader everywhere. But the Leader would be damned before he went there, to that place, with the chicks wearing the wings and playing the harps and whatever else kind of action they had going on. "I don't want to die because I won't see the people I love anymore," he used to say. Then a whole gang of the people he loved he couldn't see anymore anyhow. But that was life, as all the people said. In song, he said, "Many times I thought about cuttin' out, but my heart won't buy it." And he didn't buy it, didn't want any of those other bums to buy it, either. He told every last one of them, but they gave in or gave up or got dealt a lousy hand, which made him angry and broke his heart. Former altar boy that he was, he believed in his God, prayed always, got himself over to a Palm Springs mass whenever he could. "That forty minutes of serenity is very important in one's life," he said. But nothing much helped him with all the good-byes. He had to be by himself then, alone, the only time he ever wanted to be alone.

He preferred crying alone. "It's kind of a — it's a personal and an embarrassing moment, I think, particularly in a man, you know. . . . It's a very private kind of thing," he stammered after his mother died. From his kitchen window in Palm Springs, he could see the mountain that took her life, Mount San Gorgonio, which the kids renamed Grandma's Mountain. He'd catch himself staring at it sometimes and feel tears sting his eyes. Dolly Sinatra was a pisser, her son liked to say. No one ever gave him hell like she did — nor did anyone love him more ferociously. "She refers to me as Frank Sinatra, uses the whole name," he marveled, shortly before she left. "She wants to make sure that everybody knows who she's talking about. And I'm the only son she ever had!" For her, he would do anything, did everything she'd let him do. On January 6, 1977, he hired a plane to take her from the Springs to Las Vegas, where he was opening at Caesar's. What fell

as rain on the desert that day was ice up in the sky, blinding white; the pilot did not see the mountain. Frank could not speak for days. It should have been him, he said, not her. His father had been gone eight years, and that loss was profound. The pain of this one, however, would never heal entirely.

Dean's boy — Dean Paul Martin, young Dino — was by then a pilot-in-training. After Dolly's funeral, where his father was a pallbearer, he told Nancy Jr. what he knew of the fateful airspace: "That mountain shouldn't be there. It should be moved. It's a hazard to all pilots." Ten years later, in the cockpit of his Air Force Phantom fighter jet, Dino died on Grandma's Mountain. From that moment forward, Big Dean cared not at all about living. He sunk into what Frank called "his shell," and there he wished to stay. Frank would not let him. Within months, the Leader hatched a plan — the Together Again Tour, twenty-nine cities throughout 1988, the Pack back in celebration, gray and swinging, out to recapture all that old mothery gas. Frank told Sam: "It would be great for Dean. Get him out. For that alone, it would be worth doing." Dean told Frank, "Why don't we find a good bar instead?" He lasted one week on the road, then flew home. The amber in his glass didn't smell like apple juice anymore and he was tired, too tired to pretend it was still 1960.

Sam finished the tour with the Leader — then, a year later, they found the throat cancer. "Oh, great! I'm dying!" he said, knowing the irony. "Now Frank's gonna do another ten years onstage because I'm dying — you realize that, don't you? Frank is never going to die!" He took few visitors toward the end, but Frank was there, would be nowhere else. "You're the best friend I ever had," he told Smokey. "You're my brother." He never cried by Sam's bedside; he cried as soon as he left it. "There were times when Frank and Dad would be on the phone," says Tracey Davis, "and they didn't talk. They just held on. They really didn't have to say anything." On his tiny wrist, throughout the battle, he wore the enormous gold Cartier watch Frank gave him on the reunion tour. "It goes with me," Sam instructed his loved ones. When he went — on May 16, 1990 — the watch went with him.

HE HAD ALREADY SUNG THE PART about facing the final curtain when he fell. It had to be that song. There, in Richmond, Virginia, which Grant once took, he fell, and Richmond suddenly thought it had taken Sinatra — during "My Way," of all the goddamned things. It was March 6, 1994, a day whose dawn he had greeted after an endless night of carousal and fraternity, business as usual. Indomitable at age seventy-eight, he had put it in the bag at six-thirty that morning, slept most of the afternoon, grabbed only a cup of coffee, and gone over to the theater, which was stifling hot, airless. He fought through the show in tuxedo armor. His shirt was drenched by the time he began the song. He thought he needed to sit and pulled over his saloon stool, singing what Paul Anka wanted him to say about himself, when he blacked out, went down. The crowd gasped. Frank Jr., who conducted, stopped the music and ran over. Road manager Tony Oppedisano loosened Frank's tie, opened his shirt. He was pale, almost whiter than Suntan Charley over at the piano. Upon coming to a minute later, he asked, "What happened? Can the audience see me?" (*Dean was the one who used to gag it up and fall onstage — not him, for Chrissakes.*) They wheeled him off in a chair and he waved to the people as he went. The comic Tom Dreesen told them all that Frank was just a little warm, not to worry, to drive safely. It was dehydration, was all it was.

Backstage, the EKG said that nothing was wrong — which he knew — that his vitals were as vital as ever. Frank Jr. insisted they take him to a hospital, just to be sure. Frank said no fucking way. "Get the jet," he said.

They went to the hospital. Frank Jr. and Tony O. and Dreesen and Hank Cattaneo rode along, went into the emergency room with him. Behind a curtain, he sat on the edge of the table. Three doctors checked him again, found nothing again. Frankie told his father, "Dad, they want to keep you twenty-four hours for observation. Hospital policy. They can't release you." Frank looked at Cattaneo and said, "Is the jet ready?" The jet was ready. "Car outside?" The car was outside. Then the three doctors — internist, neurologist, cardiologist — stated their diagnoses to him one by one. Nothing seemed out of order, each said, but they would feel better if he stayed. (*They would feel better?*) Frank listened to each, thanked each for his concern, although the last guy wouldn't shut up — "Are you finished, Doc?" he said finally. The doctor said yes. "Good," said Frank. "We're gone."

It took twenty minutes to get to the plane. On board, they fixed him his Jack Daniel's immediately. He let the ice settle and lit an unfiltered Camel. He sipped and sighed.

"That's better," he said. The plane took flight, headed home for Palm Springs and the beautiful blond wife. Flying high, up there in his bird — it was his idea of nothing to do, always was.

"THIS IS BORING," he told Dean, as they helicoptered over sand and rock. This was thirty-three years before. They had been filming *Sergeants 3* out in the Utah desert with Sam and Pete and Joey. But he and Dag had an engagement at the Sands, two shows a night, so they had to fly back and forth between doing scenes. And the forty-minute copter jump each way felt like forever by the second day. *"This is boring,"* Frank kept moaning, staring down at nothing. "What do you want me to do — throw you out?" said Dean. Frank said, "Something different!" Anything. Whenever Frank was bored, he just did something else. "What bores me loses me," he liked to say. But what now? Dean had an idea: "Forget about it, tomorrow it'll be different!" he promised and said no more.

In Vegas, the next morning, Dean got up earlier than usual and went to a gun store. He bought a pair of .22s, loaded each one, hid them in his bag. Out over the desert, he pulled them out, handed one to Frank, and said, "Here, I guess you'll want to sit on the outside now. We can shoot some rabbits." Frank gave him a big grin: "You crazy bastard." How did he ever think of this stuff? He took the piece and — what the hell — began firing down at all the boring brown earth. Dean would recall, "Time just flew by, he was shooting at anything, dust, as long as he had something to do." Then Dean started shooting past Frank's face. Frank said, "You're a little close there, dago." Dean smiled that beautiful smile of his. "Hell," he said, "I don't want you to be bored, right?"

"Coo-coo," said Frank. They kept shooting at nothing. It was something to do.

An Afterword

$\mathcal{O}$nly because somebody asked, he once said, "I think my real ambition is to pass on to others what I know. It took me a long, long time to learn what I now know, and I don't want that to die with me. I'd like to pass that on to younger people." He wasn't talking about song artistry; he meant life nuance, how-to stuff, the business of comporting oneself — all of that which he has suggested only through music or private example. Two years ago, it occurred to me that he had not made good on his promise. Men had gone soft and needed help, needed a Leader, needed Frank Sinatra. So I wrote to him and appealed on behalf of manhood and mankind. I wanted to ask him essential questions, the kind that could save a guy's life. I wanted what might approximate Frank's rules of order. He took the clarion call and instructed his spokeswoman, Susan Reynolds, to gather my questions as they came in and bring them along on the road. He would sit on his plane, Jack in hand, and do what he could as an oracle, when he found the patience, a virtue he has never claimed to possess. The process took many months. Later, I was encouraged to debrief his closest confidants, who further detailed the minutiae of his ways, both then and now. (To complete the style spectrum, I did the same with intimates of Dean Martin and Sammy Davis Jr.) Supplemented as such, there emerged a composite of how the role of Sinatra is played in everyday life, whatever the circumstances. . . .

— BILL ZEHME, *Esquire*, MARCH 1996

So it began. For decades, lost men on bar stools would ask themselves the eternal drunken question: "What would Frank do?" But nobody ever asked Frank. I wrote the preceding paragraph as part of an experiment in journalism entitled "And Then There Was One . . ." Dean Martin had died two months earlier, on Christmas morning, thereby thinning the ranks of swaggering giants to within a whisper of extinction but for the one who would not let go, the one who best embodied the code to which all free-thinking men aspired, the one who wore the hats.

Never shy about sharing his beliefs, he had for the most part stopped answering questions in public forums long ago — especially in printed media, which he came to disdain. Occasionally, he responded to paper, on paper, reciting rote ponderings on the state of musical congress, then and now. This was Sinatra? I thought not — not really, anyhow. Where was the color and the bite? You had to blame the questions, which were inevitably submitted by music scholars who had gone to the foremost authority, for certain, asking him to explain the inexplicable, to deconstruct his gift with song. But what about life and what he knew of it? Arguably, no man ever lived life more broadly or confidently or stylishly than Frank Sinatra. So I sought his large legacy of mortal wisdom, plain and simple.

He was, in the end, either charmed by or merely tolerant of this idea. "It helps me pass the time," he said of the exercise, with kindly forbearance. But I was told that his face lit up on occasion when stating his policies and summoning memories. He answered nearly thirty salient questions I put forth — thus representing the last extensive interview he would give to this day. I have used almost all of his responses throughout this book — some of which appear here for the first time.

There were, however, other essential unanswered questions that required his voice. Fortunately, his voice has been endlessly captured in various media, never more candidly than on concert stages, where it is said that he spilled more autobiography in his "post time" monologues than to even his friends. Through the years, Sinatraphiles have recorded hundreds of his concerts, using methods of their own design; bundles of these tapes were made available to this project, and key nuggets of blustery smarts were carefully sifted from them. Even more invaluable were the recollections of his intimates, his family and friends, to whom he has repeated his theories of life so often that his words became indelible.

"No one knows everything about him," I was told by one of his oldest friends. Indeed, there could be no more complex figure for a writer to attempt to fully understand. The shadings of his psyche belong only to him; the life he has lived is as uncontainable as he is. This book was created not so much to report what Frank Sinatra has done but to celebrate how he did things and how he reacted to moments most human. It is part biography of sensibility, part handbook for dreamers of large dreams. "To be like Frank Sinatra," his friend George Schlatter advised, "you've got to be able to give a punch and take a punch. You've got to have a stomach like a still. You've got to be early for everything except bed. Frank is just like you. Just like me. Only bigger." Fittingly, his stories are oversized true legends, and legends are most poetic when rendered in the past tense — and so that was how this work was written. Few men deserve poetic tense as does he.

Private portals were opened in unprecedented fashion for this project, both at its inception as a magazine article and afterward. Those who know him best — who live with him, work with him, drink with him — were prevailed upon to talk about him, which does not happen, ever. Their intimate knowledge formed the portrait of the man, their stories were the palette. I am indebted especially to those who directed gates to open at the outset, who saw the wisdom of Sinatra sharing his wisdom. Furthermore, the support and kindness of Nancy and Tina Sinatra gave this endeavor renewed fortification.

Then there are the men of Sinatra, who knew his ways as well as he himself could, who traveled the world and spent years at his side: Pianist Bill Miller spent much of five decades behind him, brilliantly anticipating his whim. More recently, road manager Tony Oppedisano and concert production manager Hank Cattaneo, both beloved by their boss, were meticulous sources of unfathomable detail. The comedian Tom Dreesen, the stalwart opening act, gave generously of his time and his clarity.

Other key witnesses who spoke lovingly on the record, over the years of reportage: Frank Sinatra Jr.; Angie Dickinson; Tony Curtis; Don Rickles; Tony Bennett; Joey Bishop; Robert Wagner; Jill St. John; Steve Lawrence; Ed McMahon; the late Jackie Gleason; George Schlatter; Tracey Davis;

Sonny King; Stan Cornyn; Mort Viner; Greg Garrison; Shirley Rhodes; Armand Deutsch; Alan Livingston; Lee Solters; Garson Kanin; Marian Seldes; Arnold Lippsman; Burt Boyar; George Hamilton; Jack McHugh; Irv Kupcinet; Pepe Ruiz; Greg Field; Dana Bronson; Bill Fioravanti; Giacomo Trabalza; Jack Sepetjian and Anto of Nat Wise; and the incomparable Hollywood photographer Phil Stern, whose timeless pictures and plucky tales have informed these pages with infinite style. (It is he who belongs in a specimen jar at Harvard Medical School.) Also, invaluable audio, video, and print matter were generously donated by Dustin Doctor of the International Sinatra Society, the fan club among fan clubs (P.O. Box 7176, Lakeland, FL 33807 or http://www.sinatraclub.com); archivist Rick Apt (http://www.blue-eyes.com); Ron Simon at the Museum of Television & Radio; Mark Simone; Steve Kaufman; Tony Ocean; Ilene Rosenzweig; John C. West; John J. O'Brien; Larry S. Finley; Martha Wilson; and Gil Schwartz. No small debt is owed to certain writers who traversed this formidable subject before, some of whom actually used to drink with him: First, Nancy Sinatra, who was raised by him, wrote two essential guideposts of intimate

309

and honest observation, *Frank Sinatra, My Father* and *Frank Sinatra: An American Legend*. On the page and on the phone, she was uncompromisingly helpful (her home page: http://www.sinatra family.com). Other journalists whose work added deft perspective: Richard Gehman; Jim Bacon; Joe Hyams; Earl Wilson; Pete Hamill; Gay Talese; Nick Tosches; Arnold Shaw; Robin Douglas-Home; David Newman; and Sidney Zion, who moderated a magical night with Sinatra at Yale, in May 1986, from which several FS soliloquies have been reproduced in these pages, with gratitude.

One exceptional young journalist named Mike Thomas lent energy and brilliance to the making of this book. He is heroic and deeply talented and is now learning to drink Jack Daniel's. The indefatigible research maestro Jim Agnew sleuthed insatiably, like a truffling hound. At HarperCollins, Anthea Disney's faith meant all. And my friend and editor Mauro DiPreta inspired, waited, endured, made me better, and made this book. He is money. Molly Hennessey, at his side, of the keen eye and the wise grace, made sense of impossible men and tasks, and is also money. Paul Olsewski knew how and when to get the word out. At Sterling Lord Literistic, my agent-surfer Chris Calhoun stayed the course and made the whole world sing. His right brain, Jennifer Rockford, is hereby duked the C-note of appreciation. Endless interviews and Sinatra orations were carefully transcribed by Eugene Corey of Brave New Words (East Coast) and Genelle Izumi (West Coast). The birth of this project was presided over by *Esquire* editors David Hirshey and Michael Solomon, both of whom I miss. For moral support, there were Carrie Secrist, Christopher Pallotto, David Rensin, Richard Hull, Donna Tadelman, Rebecca Perkins, Penny Lee Hallin, Paul Brownstein, Regis Philbin, Judd Klinger, Cameron Crowe, and my fine family. For Lucy — your patience is nearly as beautiful as you are.

The employees of Thorndike Press hope you have enjoyed this Large Print book. All our Large Print titles are designed for easy reading, and all our books are made to last. Other Thorndike Press Large Print books are available at your library, through selected bookstores, or directly from us.

For information about titles, please call:

(800) 257-5157

To share your comments, please write:

Publisher
Thorndike Press
P.O. Box 159
Thorndike, Maine 04986